The 2.0 Entrepreneur

20+ Marketing Strategies for Growing Your Business Both Off and Online

Bill Corbett

The 2.0 Entrepreneur

20+ Marketing Strategies for Growing Your Business Both Off and Online

Bill Corbett

CCK Publishing, Enfield, CT

The 2.0 Entrepreneur
20+ Marketing Strategies for Growing Your Business Both Off and Online

by Bill Corbett

Published by
Cooperative Kids Publishing
P.O. Box 432
Enfield, CT 06083-0432
http://Cooperativekids.vpweb.com

Cover designed by T. Lak

ISBN-13: 978-0-9821121-5-1
ISBN-10: 0-9821121-5-7

Printed in the United States of America.

Disclaimer

This book provides information on how to use innovative 'out of the box' marketing strategies to get noticed by potential customers. It was created as a guide for those who strive to build a strong network of relationships with new, potential, and established clients and customers both off and online.

This book is sold with the understanding that the publisher and the author are not offering legal or professional services in any form.

Effective marketing requires investing time and effort into developing content, making it available, and building connections in order to develop a rewarding business. The author and the publisher in no way guarantee a lucrative business outcome simply by following the plan in this book.

All considerations have been made to make this book as complete and accurate as possible. However, there is the possibility of mistakes, omissions, or typographical errors. The text should be used as a guide and not as the ultimate or only source for growing a business. This book contains information that is current at the time of the publishing date.

The author and Cooperative Kids Publishing have neither liability nor responsibility to any person or entity with respect to loss or damage caused, or alleged to have been caused, directly or indirectly, by following the information contained in this book.

Table of Contents

Introduction

Even if you have the best product or service on the planet, without customers, you won't have much of a business. Getting the attention of customers and clients is one of the challenges entrepreneurs, consultants, sales people, and small businesses have to deal with. There is a lot of competition for people's attention. Business professionals know this, so when they receive an inquiry about their products, services, or pricing, at some point in the conversation they get around to asking "How did you learn about my products/services?" or "How did you know to call me?" The answer they get will let them know which marketing strategies are working, and help them make informed decisions about which strategies to put their money, energy, and spirit into.

Business has always worked this way. It's an exchange of one thing for another. Over the last several years though, the ways we connect with our customers and clients has been shifting and evolving, and sometimes it's hard to know exactly where we should be putting our time and financial resources. I received a call one morning from a national organization headquartered in California looking for an expert to speak at a conference. When I asked the woman how she knew to call me, she came up with a couple of possibilities, but couldn't pinpoint one specific source.

Some people would be discouraged by her response because they want immediate feedback on their marketing plan. I looked at it and realized it was one of the results of diversifying my marketing channels. For example, you probably know what Starbucks is, but can you pinpoint your knowledge of it to one specific source? Probably not. When the woman couldn't narrow down her list to one specific source, I was almost pleased because it meant that my potential customers were learning about me through my diverse marketing strategies and as a result, my business opportunities were increasing.

Gaining the attention of potential customers can be a challenge; advertising and sponsorship are incredibly expensive and don't always produce the ROI you were hoping for. Professional business growth speaker, Duane Cashin, tells his audiences that the business world is a busy, crowded, competitive space. If you want to be heard, you have to use a diverse collection of marketing channels to get your products and services noticed.

I spent nearly 25 years in the business of information technology (IT) working my way up from programmer to director. At about the halfway point through those years, I found something I became so passionate about that I decided to develop it into a business. At that time, it was considered a very unconventional line of work; certainly different from the corporate business world of my 'day job.' I had discovered my passion for helping others by speaking to them about things that could enhance, motivate, inspire and improve their lives. Soon, I was able to narrow my expertise down to sharing my passion for being a better parent, and began speaking to parents, teachers, educators, psychologists, and other appropriate audiences about how to raise cooperative and resilient children.

In some ways, building the content was easy. I was excited about my new business venture and enjoyed the research and work I had to do to create an inventory of speeches and training seminars. Figuring out how to let the world know I was ready to help them with the problems they were having raising their children wasn't quite as easy. And, whatever I did, I had to fit into the hours that were left at the end of my full time day job.

My IT career was with large financial services companies, so the marketing skills I learned and implemented there involved a limited number of marketing options delivered to a small close-knit community of existing customers. My first problem was that I didn't have an existing customer base for my new business; I had to create one. I also realized that the strategies we used from an IT perspective weren't going to help me attract new clients and customers either.

I knew I was in the middle of a world full of people who could benefit from what I had to offer, but they were all very busy and preoccupied with their lives. Typical marketing at that time was print, radio and television advertising, but I didn't have any start-up funds and those options tended to be very expensive. Still, I approached the sales department of one of the area's most popular radio stations and negotiated a price for a drive-time ad for my company and services. It cost me a few hundred dollars to get about 10 ads, 2 per day during the morning drive-time show for one week. I already had a website at the time, and I did see a slight spike in visitors during that week. I also received a few phone calls, but I knew I wasn't going to able to afford that type of advertising for very long at all.

You need deep pockets to use main stream media advertising these days and in my opinion, its effectiveness has decreased. In today's busy, congested and noisy world, effective marketing begins with two things: building a network and creating digital content; neither of which were used 20 years ago. Your network consists of the connections you make with people throughout your day, both in person, and virtually via web based social media channels. Creating digital content is the process of taking your quality offline content and putting it online in a variety of web-friendly formats so that people can more easily find you, learn about you and what you have to offer, join your network, and hopefully share your information with their network.

Combined, these two methods make up a large portion of the Web 2.0 strategies you will learn more about in this book.

Entrepreneurs understand how important it is to take advantage of today's cutting-edge marketing tools if they want to be competitive in their area of expertise. It doesn't matter if you're in the business of selling consulting services, training, insurance policies, or machine parts, you cannot expect great results if you rely on limited — sometimes outdated — marketing strategies to help you locate and connect with customers. A solid marketing plan in today's business world must include taking advantage of today's advanced techniques and technologies and all they have to offer. If you're ready to be seen and heard by a larger audience of potential customers, then start reading and learn how to become a 2.0 Entrepreneur!

Chapter 1

Don't Let The Crabs Pull You Down

When I first began sharing my dream of leaving my full time job to build my own successful entrepreneurial business, I was surprised by the response I got from family and close friends. If I mentioned my latest success at a family gathering, the topic would quickly die and then someone would step into the awkward silence and change the subject. At one event, a family member pulled me aside just to remind me that dreams like mine don't come true for most people.

I want to believe that person meant well. I'm sure his goal wasn't to see me fail or feel disappointment if my business venture didn't work out. He, like so many people, just had no idea how to support a goal he didn't understand. Few in my circle of family or friends have ever been successful at taking a dream and building it into a business.

It's the unknown that tends to bring out the pessimistic side of human nature. People who haven't successfully pursued their dreams, tend to zero in on the risks. In my circle of family and friends, I was doing something none of them had done. I was being a pioneer; in today's lingo...an entrepreneur.

Even as my cache of successes grew, there were still 'crabs' trying to dismiss my accomplishments. Feminist author and journalist, Ninotchka Rosca documented what Filipino fisherman noticed about the behavior of crabs in a bucket; when one gets close to the rim of the bucket the others seem to be grabbing its legs to keep it from escaping.

The 'crabs' in our lives are the individuals who don't deal well with anyone happier or more successful than they are. They will do or say whatever it takes to taint our success, dismiss our joy, and remind us that there's nothing special about us, or what we have to offer.

This is when it's very important to remember that we get to decide who we are. Starting anything new is a challenge and although it's difficult at times, we have the power to change the language of our self-talk so we can stay positive and keep moving forward.

When my children were growing up, I taught them a mantra-like phrase to say to themselves for inner strength whenever they were confronted by the discouraging words dished out by others. The phrase was, "No matter what you say or do to me, I'm still a worthwhile person."

As I continued to build my new business from scratch, I frequently put a similar phrase to work inside my mind. I used it to stay strong against the discouraging messages around me: "No matter what you say about my dream to build my new business, it is still a worthwhile dream, and I will remain steadfast to pursue it."

We need phrases like this to replace the ones we might have heard over and over again during our youth. If we don't create them and use them, we could end up becoming our own worst enemy, forever at the mercy of a monologue of self-limiting doubts constantly running through our mind.

In his book *Real Magic: Creating Miracles in Everyday Life*, Dr. Wayne Dyer wrote about how we all had delightful thoughts as children that let us believe we could do great and magical things. Over time though, those thoughts were replaced by thoughts that now limit us. He wrote:

> Somewhere along the way you began to doubt your ability to create magic for yourself. Never doubt that being able to walk from the perspective of the crawler is truly a miracle. You lost the ability to extend that belief to new and more 'impossible' miracles. You began to buy into the misbeliefs of

those around you who were 'many limits' people, who said, 'You must learn your limitations.' Or 'You can't do that.' Or 'You are just like your father, and he couldn't do those things either.' The list was endless, and so too became the limitations.

To recapture that childhood magic and become your own miracle worker, you will have to change the thoughts that created your world of limits and boundaries. That takes place in your mind first, and since thoughts originate with you, you have the ability to recreate your own image of what your life is going to be from now on. Why not include the presence of real magic in your life as well? (Dyer, 1989)

One of the many people who inspired me is author, professional speaker and ultra-athlete, Croix Sather, a man who followed his dream. Croix ran 100 marathons in 100 days from California to New York and inspired hundreds of adults and teens along the route. In his book *Dream Big Act Big: Breakthrough and Unleash the Superstar within You*, he wrote:

Don't EVER let anyone tell you that your dream is impossible! Nobody! Not your friends, not your parents, not your brother, sister or grandma. Certainly not that schmuck boss, or that narrow minded teacher you once had. Not that pathetic boyfriend or girlfriend whom you never should have dated in the first place. Not that moron critic or the town gossip. Nobody. Most importantly, don't ever listen to yourself when you hear those words of self-doubt creep out of the darkness of your mind. (Sather, 2011)

There is no better time than now to follow a dream and/or start a new business. For some people though, trying to figure out where to start can generate overwhelming feelings of doubt that end up stopping them from ever getting a dream or an idea off the ground. Fortunately, amazing technological advances are transforming how people connect and engage, making it easier to start new endeavors capable of changing people's lives for the better while also producing income.

This book is designed to take you step-by-step through 2.0 strategies you can use to start turning your dreams into realities, or to grow an existing business to a size that matches your goals. It will also introduce you to the advantages of adding speaking to your marketing skills portfolio.

One of the best things about all the strategies and information in this book is that they include both traditional and nontraditional, offline and online marketing strategies you can begin using immediately. With a little effort on your part, you can start doing many of them without quitting your day job. In fact, even if your dream is to start your own business, the ideas in this book might even help improve your current job situation. So, let's get started!

Chapter 2

Think Like an Entrepreneur

Like a lot of things, if deciding to follow the path of an entrepreneur was easy, then everybody would do it. They don't. There are some very good reasons to pursue this path though. One of the most important ones is because you have something worth sharing. Your experience and expertise have the potential of helping other people.

I made the commitment to pursue my goals because I knew it would allow me to live a more fulfilling life and use my gifts and passion to help others build and live a better life too.

I love what career consultant Cliff Hakim wrote in his book *We Are All Self-Employed: The New Social Contract for Working in a Changed World*:

> For most of us, it is not enough merely to survive – to change according to other people's desires or to get by on a day-to-day basis. Rather, I believe, we want to go beyond survival, not only to awaken our 'inner core' but also to live our passion, express our spirit, and make worthwhile contributions. When we are 'self-employed,' we are not cogs in a wheel, cared for by the organization, but individuals responsible for our own job productivity, career mobility, and career fulfillment. With self-knowledge, we can better identify our needs and values, build a sense of mission into our work lives, and contribute more to others. (Hakim, 1994)

If you already love what you do then perhaps you're already on the right track and just have to make a slight switch at the next 'junction.' Maybe it's time to change from working in the trenches to helping all those people who are in the trenches with you.

The reality is that too many people feel trapped in a job they hate going to everyday. Just look around you the next time you're at the grocery store, the coffee shop, or the mall. Sometimes it feels like you're living in a zombie movie surrounded by the walking dead. So many people doing the same thing day after day, existing for the sole purpose of producing for someone or something else, and once those widgets have been produced, they get their reward of returning home to the sofa and their television or computer each night. They sit there, remote control or mouse in hand feeling unfulfilled and empty, ready to give up the idea of searching for a more meaningful way of living.

In the early 1980's I began my journey as one of the walking dead. I was just out of the US Air Force and my grandmother told me I should go into the field of data processing because it promised good pay and good benefits. My grandparents were hard-working immigrants who came to this country as children. They did whatever it took to pay the bills and they did it well. But, they also complained about their employers, their jobs, the neighbors, and pretty much everything else. They weren't fulfilled and happy. Still, I had great respect for my grandmother so I took her advice.

Within a few months I found myself working for a bank, mounting magnetic reels on tape drives and loading and unloading giant reams of green and white striped paper called green-bar into humongous printers. I spent my days punching cards and bursting forms until I eventually moved into programming and from there onto management.

I'm not telling you this to fault my grandmother; she was only doing what she had been programmed to do too. Besides, I was making good money and had good benefits. I'm telling you this because back then, I didn't know it was okay to dream of being all that I was meant to be in this life. I didn't know I had a passion for consulting in the fields of behavior and parenting patiently waiting for me to find it.

One of my favorite books was written by American professor of computer science, Randy Pausch. Before dying from complications due to pancreatic cancer, he wrote his national bestseller *The Last Lecture*. It contained 61 mini-lectures providing wisdom and guidance to those who read it. My favorite lecture is the one he wrote for his own children titled *Dreams for My Children*. Here is an excerpt from that lecture:

> It can be a very disruptive thing for parents to have specific dreams for their kids. As a professor, I've seen many unhappy college freshman picking majors that are all wrong for them. Their parents have put them on a train, and too often, judging by the crying during my office hours, the result is a train wreck.
>
> As I see it, a parent's job is to encourage kids to develop a joy for life and a great urge to follow their own dreams. The best we can do is to help them develop a personal set of tools for the task.
>
> So my dreams for my kids are very exact: I want them to find their own path to fulfillment. And given that I won't be there, I want to make this clear: Kids, don't try to figure out what I wanted you to become. I want you to become what you want to become. (Pausch & Zaslow, 2008)

Fortunately, I discovered an idea that inspired me very early in my career as a young professional. The large company I was working for called all of its employees into the auditorium-like conference room to hear a presentation that was supposed to motivate us and get us excited about changes that were coming down from the new regime.

Our department head walked to the lectern and introduced the guest speaker as a leading voice in the field of innovative thinking and change. As applause filled the air, a short, bald-headed man in a suit strode confidently and quickly across the stage carrying a plastic milk crate. My attention was instantly captured by the fact that he was carrying such an odd thing until I saw what he did next; he dropped it on the floor behind the lectern and stood up on it, giving him the height he needed to stand well clear of the lectern. The entire audience immediately broke into laughter.

That was just one of the techniques the speaker used to capture our attention though. Of all of them, one technique in particular really made an impression on me and I've used it many times in my own presentations. As a means of reinforcing a point, he produced that day's local city newspaper and read the headline of an article regarding a large scale event that was meaningful to all of us in the room. What made it so memorable to me was that the speaker was from Utah and he had flown into our area just hours before taking the stage!

Yes, his message was inspiring and most likely exactly what the company's leadership wanted us to hear, but what I remembered were the things he said and did to invoke laughter from my fellow professionals. I took note of the components of his speech like the pitch and tone of his voice, his body language and how well it matched each individual message in his talk, and how well his eye contact seemed to make me feel like he was talking to me personally.

Prior to this presentation, I had sat through too many presentations that were about as engaging as watching paint dry. This speaker helped me realize that there were techniques like the milk crate and the local newspaper that could be learned and help entrepreneurs and individual thinkers stand out as the kind of professionals people want to do business with.

Something happened in my mind during that 90-minute presentation. You see... up until that moment, I wasn't exactly inspired by my job. I certainly wasn't inspired to stand up and try to get the people around me excited. Instead, I felt like my job was to fit in with the group I worked with. Standing out from the rest was not an option.

By the time I'd left that corporate auditorium though, I had witnessed the skill of a professional presenter, and experienced the energy of a truly engaged audience. And, for the first time, I was beginning to think outside the box I was currently residing in. I had just been introduced to the entrepreneurial spirit inside me and was excited and determined to learn more. I didn't know how or where to begin yet, but I made the decision to become one of those people who gets hired to motivate others, and leaves their customers inspired, informed, and moved to action. Since then, I have been on an amazing journey developing my entrepreneurial spirit and skills.

For the next several years I bought coffee or lunch for many professionals who were building their own business and were willing to share their knowledge and expertise. The most memorable cup of coffee was the one I bought for national radio talk show host, Phil Valentine, who shared many tips that I've used throughout the years. Mr. Valentine has been a featured presenter at numerous events, has written several books, has appeared in television and movies, and is considered one of the 100 most influential radio talk show hosts of all time. At the time of this writing, he was ranked as #39 according to Talkers Magazine.

I had the honor of meeting Phil when I was hosting my own weekend radio show at the Clear Channel studios in Nashville, Tennessee. We met for breakfast at the world famous Pancake Pantry restaurant on 21st Avenue in Nashville and I had the privilege of asking him many questions.

Phil generously shared many tips and ideas with me, but the one thing he really emphasized was that successful people bring their passion into their work. I've always been grateful for getting that insight so early in my career. Over the years, I've learned first-hand that people who are passionate about what they do will have the greatest impact on their clients, customers, and audiences.

In his book *PASSION! How to Do What You LOVE For a Living & Wake Up The WORLD With Your Work*, Ian Hollander describes what passion is. He writes:

> The truth is, passion is such a personal thing – an intimate exercise in expressing your authentic self... I believe whatever it is that burns brightly in you – that you'd love to get up every day and DO – is simply waiting to wake up. What you feel called to offer, or in a perfect world, simply able to do because you can.
>
> Whether you frame this a deeply "baked in" spiritual exercise in expression and authenticity that reflects something deeper about your true purpose, (as I do) or maybe you simply believe it's something purely random or chance that you happen to do well. Or maybe you have a lifelong hobby that you really love and would love to wake up and work on every day. (Hollander, 2013)

Maybe you've had the experience of realizing that there is something burning brightly in you. Maybe you've been living your parent's dream, someone else's dream, or you've become a member of the 'walking dead'. If this sounds like you, then this is the perfect time to discover new dreams or to reconnect with dreams you've been denying all along. Right now is the perfect time to reach deep inside to discover and remind yourself of all the ideas you have – or have had – that light your soul on fire.

When I decided to start pursuing my dreams, goals, and passions, it wasn't just because I wanted to pursue things I was excited about. It was also because I wanted to step off the path everyone else had chosen for me. I wanted more than an existence as someone else's employee. There's nothing wrong with working for someone else. There's just something very fulfilling about being able to take care of yourself and your family doing something you love to do.

Gratefully, one of the things I learned as I started pursuing my dream is that it's absolutely possible to grow your business without quitting your 'day job.' Jon Acuff advises in his book *Quitter: Closing the Gap Between Your Day Job & Your Dream Job*, to launch your dream job or business while you're still employed. He points out several reasons for taking this approach: it helps avoid freaking out your spouse and putting your marriage in peril, it side steps financial risks that could destroy your dream and your life, and it eliminates the loss of leverage when decisions about your new venture get tough.

An entrepreneurial business is one that can easily be started while maintaining full-time employment. This book is set up to show you how to do it, one step at a time. It may not be the only way to do it, but it's a way that has worked for many individuals, myself included. Even if the field of expertise you've chosen includes complexities that don't allow you to use all of the steps in this book, a great majority will still apply.

It should go without saying that your success is also dependent on the action you take and the effort you put into it. But if you are still trying to come up with an inspiration, here are a few questions to help you get started.

What do you love to talk about so much that when you talk about it, you feel alive? What have you discovered in your life that you'd like to share with others so that they can start living a better life too? What guilty pleasures would you love to bring out into the open?

Are there things you know how to do really well? Do you have natural talents others would love to hear about, or that you could teach? What have you learned 'the hard way'? What insight or knowledge do you possess that you could talk about right now rather than waiting until it's time for your last lecture?

Chapter3

Getting Started and
Finding Your Unique Message

To truly take advantage of 2.0 strategies, you should start by taking some time to make an inventory of your interests, the things you know about, and what entrepreneurial ideas you have that you've filed away. As a reminder though, you don't have to worry about quitting your day job to start living the life of an entrepreneur. You can start pursuing your ideas today, even if you enjoy the work you're doing now.

When it comes to selecting a business idea to focus on, passion and interest are two of the criteria you can use to narrow down your list of possibilities. Another important consideration is whether or not people will benefit from your idea. Ideas with a future usually solve a problem or address a situation people struggle with. The more defined, refined, and specific your solution is, the more likely people are to respond positively to it, and the more likely you are to stand out as an expert.

The great thing is that being an expert doesn't mean you have to be the person who comes up with all the answers. There are a lot of people out there who have figured out how to solve problems. I'm not suggesting you take credit for someone else's work and pass it off as your own, but all progress is based on the work of others. We wouldn't be able to travel by air the way we do today if it hadn't been for the Write brothers. Even if you do apply other people's ideas, you usually end up adding to them, tweaking them, or making adjustments so they fit your audience even better.

For example, I started one of my first entrepreneurial businesses in 1985. I was looking through my mail one day and noticed that I was getting pieces of advertising with my name and address printed on a stick-on label. One of them had misspelled my last name so I called the company and asked them where they got my name. The woman who answered the phone apologized and told me that the mistake probably originated at the company they were buying their mailing lists and labels from.

I didn't think about mailing lists again until I was having a conversation with the owner of a small tropical fish store in my neighborhood. He was trying to figure out a way to get customers to come to his store more often. For some reason, that misspelled address label on the piece of advertising mail popped into my head. My entrepreneurial interest took over and I quickly came up with an idea.

I asked the owner if he'd ever thought about having a giveaway contest. I explained that if he did, customers could fill out an entry blank with their name and address on it, and then he'd have the information he needed to mail advertising directly to them. He thought it was a great idea, but he didn't have a computer. Without hesitating, I told him that I had one, and for a small fee, I could do the work for him.

With that, 'Data Management and Graphics' was born and I began building mailing lists for small businesses on my brand new Commodore 64 computer – one of the first consumer computers on the market.

Today, the idea of using mailing labels on snail-mail advertising is considered by many to be old technology, but back in 1985, it was an easy way for me to earn extra income. I didn't dream up the idea of building a data base of names and addresses, I borrowed an idea that someone else had used to send me advertising. For all I know, they could have borrowed the idea from someone else too.

The point is, when you start creating your list of ideas and/or solutions, your first instinct might be that you don't know enough about one specific thing to focus on it. Nothing could be further from the truth; most people just don't realize how many things they know a lot about. Creating a list of things you already have knowledge and command of, will come from taking a good look at your skills, knowledge, experience, likes, dislikes, and passions. The bigger your initial list is, the more opportunity you will have of zeroing in on an idea that gets your creative juices flowing.

You also have an advantage I didn't have when I started. You get to start by asking yourself the right kinds of questions. Better questions make it easier to identify topics that inspire you. Jon Acuff asks his readers in his book *Quitter* to answer these five questions:

- What do I love enough to do for free?
- What do I do that causes time to feel different?
- What do I enjoy regardless of the opinions of other people?
- If only my life changed, would that be enough?
- Are there any patterns in the things I like doing?

Think about the people who inspire you. What do they talk or write about? When you go into a book store, online, or read a magazine, what kinds of ideas or information catch your attention first? Whose name would you search on the internet to see if they've written anything new lately? What kinds of things do you research on the internet?

When I decided to start a consulting business, I didn't automatically know I was going to focus on children and parenting. For me, the process evolved a little differently; it was the people I came in contact with that helped me progressively hone my skills and focus.

My close friend and co-worker, Bill Watson, suggested I join our company's Toastmasters club to develop my presentation skills. I had never heard of Toastmasters before. He explained that it is an international nonprofit educational organization dedicated to helping individuals develop their communication and leadership skills. Our company had an in-house chapter to help employees become more skilled and comfortable when they were required to speak in front of or lead work groups.

At the first meeting I attended, chapter member Clyde Talley stood behind the lectern and preceded to inspire and motivate his audience to take responsibility for their own individual emotions. With a great deal of passion, he encouraged us not to allow ourselves to be pulled down by the negative people we came in contact with on a daily basis.

The passion he spoke with made it very clear how much he believed in what he was talking about. The expression on his face, his tone, and how well his body language moved in unison with his words, it all pulled me in to listen to every word he spoke.

As strange as it may sound, I had never heard that message before. Like everybody else, I was a product of my upbringing and my experience was a circle of family and friends that reacted to whatever life tossed their way. I remember thinking to myself after hearing Clyde speak, "You mean, I don't have to let others control my emotions?!"

How long would it have taken me to figure this out if I hadn't heard Clyde's speech? How many people go through their entire lives without ever truly hearing a simple thought, idea or truth that could dramatically improve the quality of their lives in such a short amount of time? Both answers are moot because I had heard him and now I was even more determined to help other people in the same way Clyde had helped me.

Over the next few months I felt compelled to attend more and more of the club meetings. Every time Clyde spoke I saw and heard his passion. In fact, I noticed passion when other members of the club spoke about things they really cared about too. It didn't matter whether they were speaking about their children, their hobbies, or their fight down at city hall; their passion was loud and clear. You could see it in their eyes and feel it in the room.

I also wanted to hang out with these people more because they appeared just as positive and passionate in their real lives as they were when they were speaking to their audience. This was who they were as people and their positivity was contagious!

Author Jack Canfield, co-creator of the Chicken Soup for the Soul book series, said that during his first year of teaching in a Chicago High School he began to realize he didn't want to hang out in the teacher's lounge anymore. The talk always seemed to come back to topics of negativity; what the administration was doing to the teachers, judgments about the challenging students, and how difficult their jobs were going to be.

Instead, he stopped going to the teacher's lounge and discovered a different group of teachers who focused on the positive aspects of their jobs. Jack reminds us that we have the power to choose who we spend our time with. In his book *The Success Principles: How to Get from Where You Are to Where You Want to Be*, he wrote:

> Make a conscious effort to surround yourself with positive, nourishing, and uplifting people – people who believe in you, encourage you to go after your dreams, and applaud your victories. Surround yourself with possibility thinkers, idealists, and visionaries. (Canfield & Switzer, 2005)

If you're having difficulty whittling down your list of topics, begin surrounding yourself with positive people who use their passion to inspire others and distance yourself from those who generate negativity. Take an inventory of your circle of friends and family and assess whether each one encourages or discourages you.

One of the most difficult things my wife and I ever decided to do was to modify the guest list of who we invited into our home. The number of people we realized we actually enjoyed being around suddenly grew quite small. It was a difficult task to complete, but we knew it was necessary. Do the same for yourself and don't be afraid to say NO to invites from toxic people. As the amount of negativity you are exposed to starts to decrease, the things that you feel good about will start to appear and help you refine your list of topics even more.

Another thing that will help if you're still struggling with finding your message is to try spending some time alone listening for the voice inside of you that wants to guide you. Some of us think of this voice as the Greater Power and some of us call it God. It doesn't really matter what you call it, just take the time to listen. Your inner voice holds clues to what you may be passionate about.

Heather Hansen O'Neill tells us that it's important to find ways of visualizing what you want and where you believe you're supposed to be. In her book *Find Your Fire at Forty: Creating a Joyful Life During the Age of Discontent* she wrote:

> We are so often pulled in different directions that we don't know who we are or what we want. It becomes imperative to make time each day to be quiet. If you meditate or do yoga that would be optimal. But if not, simply put aside a small portion of the day to sit quietly... The habit of being quiet will help you get a clearer picture of how to live a more joyful life. (O'Neill, 2011)

In the end, it was my three children who helped me find my unique message, unbeknownst to them. After trying my hand at being a motivational speaker capable of speaking about a variety of topics, I quickly learned that there were many speakers like this. As someone once put it: "they are a dime a dozen."

I started to wonder if being a professional speaker really was the right direction for me, so I started spending time alone, in prayer and meditation to see if I could hear the guiding voice of the Greater Power inside of me. Our family began attending a new church and I watched as my children began to develop a deeper level of spirituality. As I watched them grow, an idea began to take shape and my kids were at the center of it.

After a series of enlightening conversations with my pastor, I realized how passionate I felt about being a dad and how important my relationship with my children was to me. He told me that whenever I talked about them or spent time with them he saw the 'fire in my eyes.'

My own father was absent from my life after the age of ten, and even before that, he wanted nothing to do with me or my seven younger siblings. My parents were finally and officially divorced when I was 14. That experience made me strive to be the kind of father to my children that I never had when I was growing up. I realized how passionate I was about this and started feeling like this was a better direction. I was getting closer to finding my message!

For some people, deciding on a solution they'd like to share with others is easy because they've been thinking about it for a while. For other people, it might not be as easy because it's been a long time since they've dared to think that it might be okay to do something they enjoyed and really believed in. Either way, the following exercises will help you reconnect with ideas and dreams patiently waiting to be rediscovered.

In chapter 1, I mentioned that Wayne Dyer talked about 'recapturing our childhood magic' in his book. So when we think about the things we loved to do as children, we are reminded of what it's like to think in terms of possibilities rather than limits. To remember what possibilities feel like, list five things you loved doing when you were younger – things you really looked forward to.

When I was younger, I enjoyed: _____
_____
_____

When I was younger, I enjoyed: _____
_____
_____

When I was younger, I enjoyed: _____
_____
_____

When I was younger, I enjoyed: _____
_____
_____

When I was younger, I enjoyed: _____
_____
_____

Sometimes we're unaware of all the steps we go through while we're participating in an activity we really enjoy. But just because they are second nature to us doesn't mean they are as obvious to everyone else. In this exercise, write down at least 3 skills or 3 pieces of information other people would have to have to proceed with the activities you listed above. For example, if you really enjoyed hiking when you were young, 3 things people might want to know are: how to prepare for climbing their first mountain, what kinds of food are best to take on the trail, and first aid for hikers.

Skills and/or information people would need to _____
_____are:
1._____
2._____
3._____
Skills and/or information people would need to _____
_____are:
1._____
2._____
3._____
Skills and/or information people would need to_____
_____are:
1._____
2._____
3._____
Skills and/or information people would need to_____
_____are:
1._____
2._____
3._____
Skills and/or information people would need to_____
_____are:
1._____
2._____
3._____

By now, even if you haven't made an absolute decision about what you want to share, your mind is starting to expand with ideas. This is how every entrepreneurial success starts – with an idea. The more passionate and exciting the idea is to you, the more likely you are to engage your audience.

For this exercise, think of 3 people who inspire you and make you want to get up and do something every time you see them, hear them, or read something they've written. What do you think their message is? What is it about them that inspires you?

1. I am inspired by: _____
Their message is: _____
_____
They inspire me to: _____
_____

2. I am inspired by: _____
Their message is: _____
_____
They inspire me to: _____
_____

3. I am inspired by: _____
Their message is: _____
_____
They inspire me to: _____
_____

Chapter 4

Developing Yourself as an Expert

As an entrepreneur, you get to extend your reach and share your message directly with your audience of potential customers knowing it has the power to improve or inform some aspect of their lives. To better position yourself as an expert known for your valuable advice, coaching, or training, you will need to combine your passion with one another quality that will help you rise above all the other voices and get you paid in the process. You need to become an expert in the topic you've chosen.

The dictionary defines an expert as someone who has special skills or knowledge. In his book *KaChing: How to Run an Online Business that Pays and Pays*, Joel Comm says that EVERYONE is an expert. He writes:

> Everybody is an expert in something because everyone has to fill 24 hours of his or her day with something. Even if you spend half of that time on the sofa watching television and the other half in bed sleeping, then you're an expert on sofas, daytime soaps, and a dozen ways to waste your time. (Comm, 2010)

In 1995, with my expertise in mind, I began searching the web to see what other experts in parenting and child behavior were getting paid to talk about. I stumbled on a website about positive parenting and found out they were offering training classes at various locations around the country for individuals who wanted to become certified positive parent trainers.

It didn't take me long to figure out that this training would be an amazing opportunity to develop positive parenting skills as a dad to my three children. The bonus of becoming certified to teach others how to be positive parents would also add to my credibility as an expert on the subject.

When it comes to educating yourself on your chosen topic, Dottie and Lilly Walters say that we can never know enough about a topic we want to become an expert on. They suggest constantly increasing knowledge in the subject. In their book *Speak and Grow Rich* they said:

> Having a degree is not essential to being a highly paid professional speaker. Having the knowledge that goes with the diligent study is! Look for classes that are flexible enough for you to do your studying on the road. (Walters & Walters, 1997)

One of the best resources for low-cost training is your local community college or community education center. Working on a degree in your topic area is certainly ideal, but not always necessary. Many colleges have noncredit training centers where all sorts of classes offer training for soft skills, technical skills, and even specialized skills, and all at reasonable prices.

You may be fortunate and already have an academic background related to your chosen topic. If you do, it's a good foundation for your list of credentials. But, formal education alone won't always compensate for a lack of experience. That's okay though, because becoming an expert isn't just the result of a formal education. Sometimes the most impressive credentials we have are the ones we earned by successfully making the journey through life's challenges.

A woman I crossed paths with was also pursuing a career as a consultant on child behavior and discipline. She possessed several high-level degrees related to her topic but was not a parent herself. When speaking to a group of parents one day, someone from the audience asked her if she had children of her own. She didn't, but she did have the kind of real life experiences that would qualify. She quickly replied no and then proceeded to reveal that she had many years of experience as a children's camp counselor, a Sunday school teacher, and as an aunt to her nieces and nephews.

If there's a risk that you may appear to lack the kind of experience someone might expect, write down a list of all of your past experiences: jobs, hobbies, association memberships, volunteer opportunities, and other life experiences. Examine each one to look for anything that could even remotely be related to your topic and capture that information for future use.

Another way to acquire practical experience is to be of service to organizations in your area. Local and non-profit organizations are always looking for volunteers and/or board members. I received a call from my local sheriff's department one day, asking me if I was willing to come in and talk to incarcerated fathers. Someone had heard about my work with parenting and had given them my name as a speaker. It was a little frightening at first but ended up being an incredible experience.

I heard of an organization that provided classes for pregnant teens and teenage parents at a local high school. I contacted them and offered my services free of charge. They were excited about my offer and I provided several workshops for them and their clients.

Working with a variety of groups has given me the invaluable experience and opportunity to better understand the challenges of parenting from many different perspectives. It has added to the collection of stories I use to back up points in my talks (minus names and other personal information of course) and more importantly, it has increased my credibility with my audiences of potential customers.

If you aspire to be a consultant on cats or dogs, offer to volunteer down at your local animal shelter. If your message is related to teen dating violence or relationships, community domestic violence units are always looking for volunteers. If your dream is to provide solutions on programming or the use of computers, offer to give classes at your local senior center or teach classes at a community education center.

We live in an amazing world where education and experience can be acquired in so many different ways. Even the web provides an almost unlimited amount of information, education, and opportunity to beef-up your expert credentials.

As your topic begins to take shape, drill deeper to find the message you want to share. Determine which aspects of your message you have complete confidence in and seek out education and experiences that will fill out the rest. Become the kind of expert that will have a positive influence on people. And for the best experts/speakers around, this never ends; it becomes a way of life. Dotty and Lilly Walters said:

> Speakers are booked because they are experts: experts at humor, motivation, or with information and insight in a specific area of knowledge. Today expertise is much more easily accessible by the average person than it was even five years ago. Online systems, phone hookups, and video conferences open a floodgate of information to anyone. Therefore, to be competitive with the average ten-year-old it becomes even more important for you to be on top of the information pertinent to your field of expertise. (Walters & Walters, 1997).

What expertise are you ready to develop in yourself? Everyone can become an expert and don't let others make you think differently. I've seen people (myself included) with degrees, certificates, awards, and amazing accomplishments get cut down and berated by those who've questioned an entrepreneur's status as an expert despite all the evidence presented. Those doing the berating do it for reasons you will probably never know and don't need to know because their reasons probably have nothing at all to do with you. Sometimes it's just easier for people to dismiss what you have to offer than it is to face their own problems.

Only you can share your message. There might be other people who consult on similar things, but you do it from your experience with a passion that is uniquely yours. It's this unique combination of experience, education, and passion that will inspire your audience.

Chapter 5

Developing Talks that Lead to Sales

Whether your position involves direct sales or indirect selling, one of your major business goals is moving your customers and clients to take action. It doesn't matter if your job is to educate them from the stage as a speaker or trainer, help them solve a problem face-to-face as a consultant or customer service rep, or convince them to purchase your product or service as a direct sales professional. Each of these scenarios requires taking what you know and turning it into content that will help you build a relationship with both current and potential customers and clients.

Daniel Pink, author and former chief speech writer for Vice President Al Gore, wrote in one of his latest books that just about all professionals are in the business of sales, or as he puts it, 'non-sales' selling. After commissioning a survey to find out how much time people were spending on moving others to take action, Mr. Pink discovered that business people were spending about 40% of their time on activities designed to persuade and convince others to give up their resources. He also learned that these activities were critical to their businesses' success. In his book *To Sell Is Human: The Surprising Truth About Moving Others*, he wrote:

> Once upon a time, only certain people were in sales. Every day, these folks sold stuff, the rest of us did stuff, and everyone was happy. One day, the world began to change. More of us started working for ourselves—and because we were entrepreneurs, suddenly we became salespeople, too. (Pink, 2012).

Some days you might be addressing a room full of potential clients; other days you might be standing in front of just one decision maker. Either way, you are selling yourself, your business, and your products. Thinking like an entrepreneur means understanding that this is as much about marketing as it is about content. Preparing for these occasions by taking the time to develop your content into polished presentations, pitches, and speeches will ultimately lead to more business and increased sales regardless of what line of work you're in.

Developing Content for Your Talks

You can start building and organizing your content in a variety of ways. Because you've been working on narrowing your topic in addition to expanding your education, you already have a good idea of what you want to talk about. One of the easiest ways to start getting it down on paper is to ask yourself, "What do I know about my topic at this point?"

By making a list of everything you know about your topic, you are providing yourself with an inventory of options. Not everything on the list will make it into every talk, but having a large selection of points, information, ideas, strategies, etc. to choose from will help you build a well-rounded outline. When you think you're done, look at your list again and continue to break entries down until each entry is its own unique point.

Post-its™ are great for building outlines. As you start examining your list, groupings of ideas will start to take shape. Write individual entries down on their own post-it and start organizing them in the same order you would use to explain them to someone. This method is both a visual and tangible way to organize a rough outline. It will also highlight any gaps in your knowledge or information, and help clarify the direction for continuing your education. If you feel like you lack enough information to flesh out your topic, that's just another reminder that there's almost always more to learn.

When I started building content, I knew that my general topic was parenting. As I narrowed the topic down, my niche message became focused on challenging behaviors in young children. Once that decision was made, I set out to learn all I could. I asked myself, "What can I learn about these challenging behaviors and what causes them."

I began to read all the books I could find on children and child behavior. At that time it was the mid-1990s and parenting was just beginning to become a topic for books. The information I found while searching libraries and bookstores was generally written by psychologists and pediatricians, and tended to be very clinical in nature.

Start With Understanding Who Your Audience Is

From there, I started to think about my audience; who were they and what challenges were they facing? Ask yourself, "Who will have the greatest interest in what I have to say?" Envision a room full of people all sitting quietly listening to your message. Who are they and what would bring them all together? If it's hard to think of a group of people, start by thinking about one person sitting at your kitchen table listening intently because he or she wants to hear every word you have to say. Who is that person? How old are they? What do they do for work?

The better you understand your audience, the easier it will be to design your content so that it answers their questions and provides them with useful and meaningful information. People don't want a speech; they want a solution to a problem they need to solve.

Seek out individuals or groups appropriate for your topic and ask them what their top three problems in your topic area are. Check internet forums and look through the questions people ask. If, like me, your passion was born out of your own personal experience, rethink your past in terms of your topic. What questions were you asking then, and how would the expert in you answer them now?

As a father of three children, I had experienced challenges I could use to start building content. I wanted to get more cooperation from my children; I wanted solutions to address power struggles and I needed some tools to help me with sibling rivalry and fights. In the process of coming up with solutions to each of those problems, I created content for three different talks: "How to Get Kids to Cooperate More," "How to Stop Tantrums," and "How to Handle Sibling Rivalry."

Once I had a collection of answers that had solved my problems, I also had a strong sense of empathy for the people who would be sitting in my audience. They would be experiencing the same problems I had dealt with. Now they would be listening to me hoping the content I presented would solve one or more of their problems.

Focusing and identifying your target audience's problems and then building content that provides solutions is a great way to think about your content.

Validate Your Solution

Before I was ready to present my solutions to an audience though, I wanted to have them validated. Whenever I met a parent and it was an appropriate opportunity, I would run my solutions by them and ask them if they thought these solutions would be helpful to them with their parenting. Most everyone I talked to liked the solutions I offered. A couple parents even volunteered additional problems they were struggling with: "How do I get my children to listen to me" and "How do I get my kids to care about school." Those two problems and their solutions combined with my original three problems and their solutions became the basis for my first five speech topics.

Once you have an outline in hand, you are ready to do two things. The first thing is to start composing your talk. Take each item in the outline and expand it so that when you are talking about it or explaining it, you will be giving all the information someone might need to understand and implement your ideas and strategies.

Fleshing out each point as much as you can in the beginning can make the difference between talking at people, and sharing your solution. When you take the time to really expand your content, you will be providing your potential customers with enough information so that when they leave they will have a plan to follow, the inspiration to follow it, and a belief that there is a way to solve their problem.

The second thing you can do with your expanded content is to use it as a guideline for marketing yourself. Using the outlines I built for my first presentations as a reference, I created a brief list of bullets that revealed the highlights of each presentation and then posted the information on my website. I also created a one-page flyer with a concise description of each presentation. These I was able to hand out to audiences after a presentation, send out to potential clients, and use as part of my marketing/press kit (we will cover this in a later chapter).

Being able to give specific information about the content of your talks to potential clients is always an advantage. Being specific about what you have to offer also avoids the awkward situation of having a potential client ask you to speak on a topic you aren't knowledgeable about. The bottom line is that if your content isn't organized well enough for you to explain it to a potential client, it's going to be a bigger challenge for you to sound like an expert and a professional.

The point is: your content is the foundation of your entrepreneurial career. Take the time to gather and organize your quality content; it will help you earn your expert credentials more quickly, and move you one step closer to getting a glowing recommendation from a customer.

Chapter 6

Honing Your Speaking Skills

Over my 20 years as a professional I have learned a great deal about professional presenting and speaking techniques from many different sources. Before I found my passion for speaking to an audience full of potential customers though, I thought about speaking the same way a lot of people do; it looks really scary, but I'll never have to do it. Boy was I wrong!

My first presentation took place early in my career. It was true that I had never spoken in front of a group before, but making presentations to managers and co-workers was part of my job now. And yes, I had seen the Toastmasters posters around the building, but speaking to a bunch of people I work with didn't really seem like public speaking. Like I said, it was just another job requirement.

I honestly thought I had done a good job preparing. I had planned out the material I would be presenting well in advance and practiced the talk throughout that week. As the date of my presentation got closer, I felt a mixture of excitement and nervousness which I hoped was a good combination. The excitement would provide courage, and the nervousness would help keep my feet on the ground. What could go wrong? Everything!

On the day of the presentation I felt okay, but as the appointed hour approached, my nerves began to get the better of me. When it was time for me to give my presentation, I stood on the side of the room listening to my introduction and as I walked to the front of the large conference room, a whole bunch of physiological changes started to unfold.

First, the intensity of my nervousness was quickly turning into panic. Too nervous to make eye contact, I looked at the sheet of paper I was holding in one hand and realized my hands were trembling. My knees started to tremble too, and I had the odd sensation of them going numb. Now, I was frozen with the additional fear that I might actually fall down!

I tried to divert my attention away from my body by looking at the index card notes I held in the other hand, but the words looked blurry and I couldn't read them. I tried to put sentences together based on what I could remember about my topic, but my mind seemed to go blank. Needless to say, my first presentation in front of my department was a complete disaster!

Somehow, I managed to string enough ideas together to get through the presentation and was very relieved to hear applause as I took my seat. In retrospect it was probably 'pity applause,' but all I heard was applause and I was in no condition at that moment to judge the intent of my audience. When I had the time to calmly dissect how the talk really went, I realized there might be more to speaking than standing up in front of people just because you have something to say.

It was shortly after my first attempt at giving a presentation that I heard my first real motivational speaker – the one who stood on a milk crate. On my trip to the company cafeteria the next day, I stopped at one of the bulletin boards and looked for the Toastmasters poster. The co-worker I was with saw me looking at it and said he would never go to those meetings because they make people stand up and talk in front of the group. I thought to myself – how much worse could it be than what I'd experienced with my presentation?

Toastmasters—A Top Development Resource

I owe a lot to Toastmasters and all the other organizations and people who helped teach me about the physical aspects of the speaking part of being in business. I began to enjoy attending club meetings because I was always learning something about speaking and about who I was as a speaker.

We are all ego-centric to some degree, but when we start something new – like speaking – we can easily get stuck in our own head and in our own narrow perception of how we think we appear to others. Participating in a speakers group provides an opportunity to be evaluated in a respectful and informative way by other speakers. It's a way for us to develop an inner awareness of how our perception of ourselves on stage might differ from the perception of the audience.

At the risk of sounding like a paid advertisement, Toastmasters International is probably one of the best-kept secrets for entrepreneurial success in the world. With thousands of chapters across the globe, this nonprofit international organization offers self-paced education and training in the areas of communications and leadership to any adult seeking greater success in their professional and personal lives. I recommend chapter membership to anyone seeking success in any career.

After my first few months as a member of my company's Toastmasters chapter, I wasn't quite as nervous at staff meetings or with presentations. Co-workers told me they had noticed differences in my presentations, and it felt really great to get positive feedback about my progress.

Remain Open to Learning

I realized very quickly that there were a few types of people who joined Toastmasters. There were those who joined and stayed just long enough to accomplish some type of personal goal – like being able to present in front of a group at work, or to give a toast at a wedding. There were people who enjoyed the opportunity to speak about subjects that mattered to them. And then there were people like me who believe that there's always an opportunity to learn more about what we've chosen to do.

Some people believe that because they are experts with years of experience within their chosen fields, they are ready to add speaking to their business without any training. One of their friends or a colleague might tactfully suggest investing in a speaking class to improve their public speaking skills, but the kinds of speaking skills every speaker should strive to develop aren't acquired by the end of one public speaking course or after a couple of months with a speaking organization. Skills grow and develop over time every bit as much as we grow and develop over time.

Learning is an ongoing process no matter what skill or knowledge you're trying to develop. Brendon Burchard, author of *The Charge*, writes about the many benefits of being a lifelong learner:

> The desire to learn and master our lives is critical to our confidence and happiness. If we approach learning with joy and enthusiasm, we tend to feel more confident and capable in life. And neuroscientists are now proving that the more we learn, the more our neural pathways strengthen, which leads to our ability to better anticipate and perform, which in turn leads to the pleasurable releases of dopamine in the brain. (Burchard, 2012)

When it comes to the business world, there are two acquired skills that are associated with top-notch, in-demand experts: a thorough knowledge base from which to present to potential clients, and the skill to present that knowledge in an informative and interesting format. These two skills are important regardless of whether you are just starting out or have 20, 30 or more years as an expert in your field. All professionals have the same goal; to give their presentation more than once.

If you want to get hired as a leading expert in your field, muster up the courage and take the time to seek out the advice of other professionals to get a better understanding of whether or not your knowledge, information, and skills as a presenter are as obvious to your audience as they are to you. Allow yourself to be evaluated at Toastmasters meetings, public speaking classes or have someone video tape your presentations. Each of these is a great opportunity for getting feedback.

It's true that feedback isn't always comfortable. Recently I had the task of providing feedback to a business associate who was also a friend. It was hard because she was just starting out as an entrepreneur and she just completed her first big presentation. It was also hard because the feedback from the client wasn't very good.

She took it fairly well but struggled to understand some of the issues because she was still thinking about her experience at the front of the room from her perspective rather than from the audience's perspective of her. I asked her to try and focus on the feedback as an opportunity to learn.

In this respect, human beings are very much alike. Our first instincts are to protect ourselves by ignoring and/or rejecting feedback. We might also feel like we need to defend ourselves. We'll perk up and listen to positive feedback, but if it's constructive, it doesn't always matter how well it's delivered, our first reaction is very often defensive.

This is when we need to remind ourselves of the benefits of listening to other people's interpretations of our work. We have something we want to share with people to help them with a specific problem, issue or situation. What's more important: learning how to successfully share our information with an engaged audience, or the temporary ego bruise that results from realizing we have more to learn?

Bottom line: take advantage of opportunities to continue learning and growing as a professional. If there comes a time when you really just need to hear how great you are, take your best friend out for lunch. Talk about how hard you are working and that person will very likely give you the kind of ego boost we can all use once in a while.

As I did with my friend, I urge you to replace the automatic response to defend yourself with a conscious decision to always be engaged in learning and self-improvement. In his book *The 7 Habits of Highly Effective People*, Stephen R. Covey used the metaphor of 'sharpening the saw' to explain the 7th habit:

> Suppose you were to come upon someone in the woods working feverishly to saw down a tree. "What are you doing?" you ask. "Can't you see?" comes the impatient reply. "I'm sawing down this tree." "You look exhausted!" you exclaim. "How long have you been at it?" "Over five hours," he returns, "and I'm beat! This is hard work." "Well, why don't you take a break for a few minutes and sharpen your saw?" you inquire. "I'm sure it would go a lot faster." "I don't have time to sharpen the saw," the man says emphatically. "I'm too busy sawing!" (Covey, 1989)

Stephen Covey's 7th habit made such an impression on me that I made a commitment to myself to remain actively involved in self-development forever.

You will meet and hear about people who think they have the best selling or speaking skills in the world and claim to be booked solid, week after week. It might be true, but even they will eventually end up in a rut if they don't continually make an effort to 'sharpen their saw.' Every successful professional, regardless of their chosen field, is always open to learning more. It's one of their secrets for staying at the top.

Forget the idea that you already know all you need to know about either your topic or your presentation skills. Stay open to the idea that there's always room to improve and grow. Be grateful for your passion and your message and commit to learning as much as you can about both from this point forward. In the end, the more informed you are about your topic and the more skilled you are at sharing your message, the more engaged and inspired your potential customers will be.

Chapter 7
Setting up Your Portable Office

So far, we've talked about a host of different strategies for building content and establishing yourself as an expert both off and online. Individually, each of the strategies covered employs a different method for extending your reach. Combined, they share a common goal: creating multiple opportunities for getting noticed, recognized, and hired.

Whether your goal is to launch a new business or a side business as an expert, a consultant, or an entrepreneur, there are things you can do to start building your business while still working your day job. In this chapter we will cover how to prepare for those first phone calls and emails from new and potential clients.

The Business Card

You don't always know when you're going to be making a first impression with a potential client. It might be face-to-face at a networking event, a conference, or at an organizational meeting. It might also be in the produce aisle of your local grocery store.

One of my opportunities came from a chance meeting while I was shopping. It was initiated by a woman who recognized me from one of my public events. She approached me, told me she was a therapist, and was very interested in my work. She also told me she had been considering recommending me as a speaker to get in front of an audience for an event she was involved with.

After a few minutes of conversation, she asked me for my business card and I asked her for hers. One of the first lessons I learned early in my entrepreneurial career was to always be prepared to meet my next client, so I try my very best to always have at least one business card with me. I handed her my card, but she had to admit that she didn't have any with her. She said: "Wow, you're really prepared." If I hadn't had a card on me, would she still have recommended me? Possibly, but by being able to give her my contact information right then and there, I was able to present myself as a professional, always prepared to do a great job.

When you're starting your business, you don't want to give a potential client any reason to doubt your ability to deliver, especially if this is your first introduction to them. When someone asks you for a business card and you don't have one, it might send the message that you're not quite ready to step into the professional arena. Professionals carry business cards with them because they want the people they meet to know they are ready, willing, and able to provide the services they are offering.

When it comes to the card itself, the number one tip is: don't skimp. There is nothing that screams AMATEUR! as much as a flimsy card with perforated edges or the printer's trademark on the back. Take the time to design a business card that represents the professional you aspire to be, the professional you want to present to your perfect client. You can check out printing websites for samples; you just might find your perfect card already designed. You can also check out local printers in your brick and mortar community. Either way, once you have your professional business cards in hand, always make sure you have them in your pocket too.

Selecting Your Business Card Information

In an ideal business world, we'd all be able to meet our potential clients face-to-face and have the opportunity to make our best first impression. Business doesn't work like that though, and sometimes it's your business card that will be making that first impression for you. Consider all the different ways people in the business world contact each other and decide how many contact options you want to list on your card. Take the time to organize the information so it's easy to read.

Phone Numbers

Phones are an interesting subject these days because of the choices we have. Cell phones are here to stay, but home phones? Some people have decided to ditch their home phones and go strictly with cell phones.

On your business card, you want a phone number that people can use to call you and speak with you directly about your business. This doesn't necessarily mean you need to bring another landline into your home to accommodate your new business phone. It does mean you'll want to have at least one phone number dedicated to your business.

Think about your current situation. Are you going to be moving in the near future? If you move will you be able to take the business phone number with you? One of the advantages of cell phones is that you can usually keep your phone number even if you do move or change carriers.

However you decide to set it up, think long term because you want your contacts to always be able to get in touch with you. Changing phone numbers every few months means losing contacts because if the number on your card is out of service, they are just going to assume you're out of service too.

Once you've made your decision and have a business phone number, make a personal commitment to always answering it professionally rather than with an informal "Hello?" Whenever my business phone rings, I answer it saying, "Hi, this is Bill Corbett. How can I help you?" You want your potential clients to believe from the very start that they are dealing with a true positive professional.

Selecting a Professional Email Address

Email is never going to replace the telephone as a key method of contact in the business world, but it does increase the ease with which we are able to interact with other professionals. In some ways, email is a way to respect how busy people are. Emails are less intrusive; when a phone rings, it interrupts. Emails sit and wait patiently until you are ready to check them. And, because email accounts are so easy to set up, I suggest having a business email address that is separate from your personal email address and your day job email address.

Many people still have the personal email address they started with years ago. They include initials, numbers, and even pet names. It's hard to convince someone of your professional status when your email address is something like: honeybun549@hotmail.com. Instead, set up a separate email address for corresponding with anyone tied to your new business adventure.

There are two primary ways of obtaining an email address for your speaking business. Your first option is to choose one of the *free* email services you'll find on the internet.

Email Option #1:

There are many free email providers on the internet, but today, the four primary ones are: Yahoo, Google, Hotmail and AOL (America Online). You can acquire a free email address at any of these providers by going to their website and signing up for a free account. For example, to get a Google email account, you will type www.gmail.com in the URL window of your internet browser. When their site appears, click on **Create an Account** and the site will lead you through the steps of creating an account. Your email address will have their name at the end.

Email Option #2

Your second option is to set up your email with the same

domain registrar you used to secure the website URL you picked for your business. This provides a more professional looking email address that ends with your business URL. For example, one of my websites is www.BillCorbett.com. Anyone interested in emailing me can send an email to: bill@billcorbett.com. Because I used NameCheap.com as my registrar and web host, I had access to that email address as soon as I purchased the domain name.

You can check with your domain registrar to see what they offer for email services. If they only offer one free email address, you might want to consider moving your URL to a different web hosting service with more options.

Voicemail

Once you've decided on your 'official' phone number, you're going to want to set up your professional voicemail greeting. Take your time with the greeting so that people will hear a quality recording letting them know they've reached your business. It should go without saying that if you're in the middle of a business meeting, or otherwise occupied, let incoming calls go to voicemail. In fact, if you're in a meeting, think about turning your cell phone off; the one exception being when you are waiting for a call specific to your current conversation.

I once made a phone call to someone I was interested in hiring for a particular service. This person had been highly recommended by an acquaintance, but when I called the number on his business card, he answered with "Hello?" I told him who I was and what I wanted to talk about. He sounded a bit annoyed for some reason and then said to me, "Can I call you back? I'm out with another client right now."

I told him I'd call him back and hung up. I never called him back, and he lost any future business from me for sure. The lesson here is: if you can't take the call, don't answer it. Let it go to voicemail. A professional will always prefer your undivided attention to being made to feel like an intrusion.

Returning Phone Calls and Email Messages

When it comes to returning calls and messages, promptly is always the best method. If too much time lapses between their initial contact and your response, you'll have given them both the time and a reason to consider your competition. People have deadlines to meet and it's very likely they won't wait around for you to get back to them.

The biggest advantage to prompt responses is that then you don't have to come up with an excuse for the delay in your reply. For me, there are three excuses I hate to hear. The first one is "I've been busy" and the second is "I haven't had the time." When you tell someone you've been too busy to respond, it's like you're telling them that your time is more valuable than theirs. We are all given the same amount of time every day. Saying that you haven't had the time to respond will make them wonder if you'll have the time to meet their deadlines or to show up on time.

What is an acceptable response time? Anywhere between as-soon-as-possible and the end of business the following day. This time frame accommodates a variety of situations. People generally have a chance to check their messages by the time they go to bed. When they don't check them at night, then they'll probably check them first thing in the morning. If you want to be considered a professional, you need to add checking your messages to your schedule. If you find that you are having problems responding within an acceptable time frame, then maybe it's time to take an honest look at your time management skills.

Even when you are doing your best though, there will be times when a delay is unavoidable. That's when my third least favorite excuse, the 'Too Much Information' story, usually comes into play. Things happen in life. When they do, simply apologize for the delay without making or offering excuses. If you find that your normal response time is usually longer than 24 hours, let people know in your voicemail, or tell them when you meet them.

Sometimes a delayed response is due to circumstances that regularly interfere with your ability to respond – like when you still have your day job. If your current situation makes it hard for you to respond within a reasonable amount of time on a daily basis, consider hiring an assistant to return calls and emails on your behalf. Over the years, I've used high school students, stay-at-home moms, and even college interns to help me run my business.

Other times a delayed response is for no other reason than your genuine nervousness about how you will come across on the phone. The solution? Practice. Think about the questions you're afraid people are going to ask, come up with answers, and practice saying them out loud until you can comfortably 'recite' your responses.

The goal, when it comes to responding to voicemails and emails, should be to manage them in a consistent and professional manner. This way, over time your clients will come to know what to expect from you. That in turn enhances the development of your relationship with them.

Section II

Chapter 8

Getting Your Content Online

In many ways, starting a career as a consultant, sales professional, or entrepreneur is just like starting any other career. In addition to education, there are a variety of tools at your disposal that can help you expand your reach and increase the size of your audience. In chapter 5, we covered ways of creating and organizing your content into an inventory of talks, presentations, and speeches. In this chapter we will be talking about how to build your online presence so that people will have multiple opportunities for finding you and taking advantage of what you have to offer.

Do you absolutely need a web/social media presence to build a successful business? Yes, you do. Thanks to computers, the World Wide Web, the internet, Web 2.0 tools, and all those brainiacs working hard to make it all easier to understand and use, you can connect and develop relationships with professionals and potential clients regardless of their physical location. People are searching for knowledge, information, solutions, etc., 24 hours a day, 7 days a week. Think of what it can mean to a person living on the other side of the planet when they find answers, ideas and solutions to their problems, just by finding you online.

Accepting new things and liking them can be challenging. Change often requires learning new skills as well as how to apply those new skills even when you're feeling like your time and focus are already stretched to the max. If your goal is to develop yourself as an entrepreneur and expert, you're going to want to embrace Web 2.0 strategies because many of your potential customers are already using them. The web is full of opportunities to go where your customers are instead of waiting and hoping they will call you, snail mail you, or run into you somewhere outside your office.

If you've already learned how to use Web 2.0 on your own, or as part of your day job, then this chapter will encourage you to think about how you can use these tools to your advantage as an entrepreneur. To those of you who haven't gotten online with a website or engaged in social media yet, I can tell you that I was in your shoes once and now wish I'd embraced the internet and all it has to offer sooner.

Several years back, I remember getting scolded by my oldest daughter. She warned me that I needed to have a MySpace page to promote myself as a parenting consultant. She was right and I ignored her warning way too long.

MySpace was one of the first popular social media sites. My original perception of it, and of all those other new social media sites, was that they were just another time-wasting fad people were flocking to because it was popular. I was also thinking about how old my daughter was compared to how old a potential client of mine would be. It was hard for me to believe that adults and reputable business people were using MySpace. Now I know that if I had been smart enough to take her advice back then, I'd likely have a much larger platform now.

The web has come a long way since then and there are many more options to choose from now. As your comfort and skill level expand, you'll be able to decide which channels and tools you like working with the most. If you're just starting out though, the recommendations provided here are guidelines based on my own personal experience combined with suggestions from a variety of other Web 2.0 gurus.

One of the biggest advantages to building your online presence is that it allows you to market yourself to a much larger audience than you could possibly contact on your own. Being online means that people can find you. It can also free up some of the time that you would otherwise be spending on cold-call marketing.

Of all the business opportunities I've secured over the years, my two highest paying were the result of someone finding me online. The one that paid me $10,000 for a two day training session was the result of an organizer working with parent educators and social workers finding my website. Her organization had just secured a grant to assist parents in the community with their children. The information she read on my website inspired her to call me and interview me over the phone. Within a couple of weeks, I was on a plane headed to another part of the country to speak and train a large group of parent educators.

Many of my past opportunities were the result of referrals coming from someone finding my website or social media posts while they were doing internet research. They liked what they read about me and what I do, and then passed my information along to someone they knew who was looking for an expert. In other words, the person who found me on the internet forwarded to, or shared my information with, another person via the internet.

Any way you look at it, the internet is here to stay. Websites and social media are here to stay too and will only develop and evolve as time goes on. It's hard to say which brand name Web 2.0 channels will remain and for how long, but it's important to get on board now to take advantage of your opportunity to get found and get noticed.

Websites

A website is one of the most fundamental ways to establish your presence on the internet. It's your online *real estate*; a place where anyone can go to learn more about you and your expertise. Clients often begin their search on the internet. Having a website increases your chances of being found by individuals looking for information or services in your field of expertise.

Your website doesn't have to be elaborate, but you'll want to take the time to make sure it looks professional. When people find it, it will be their first introduction to you and what you have to offer. In the same way that we tend to make decisions about people based on their personal appearance, people will think of your website as a reflection of you.

It is possible to build a website without the help of a professional, but this might be one of those things you should consider spending some money on to make sure it looks polished, positive and professional. If it doesn't, potential clients will leave your page and look at what your competitors have to offer instead.

In 1984, Jay Conrad Levinson started talking about 'guerrilla marketing.' While the term might have been around for a while, his series of books and their consistent message to 'think outside the box' continues to apply to marketing a small business even today. Here's what Jay had to say in his book *Guerrilla Publicity*:

> Your Website is the first resource that prudent potential customers, clients, or peers examine to find out more about you and your product or service. It speaks directly to the business you want to attract – innovative businesses that are blazing trails into the new millennium. It shows that you're a kindred spirit, a player in the twenty-first-century economy. It also tells them who you are, what you're doing, and where you're headed. Remember, most people prefer doing business with people who are on the same wave length. Don't you? (Levinson, Frishman, & Lublin, 2002)

There are many books and websites out there that can guide you through the process of building your own website if you want to give it a shot. You can go to YouTube, type the words *build a website* into the search box, and you'll find a slew of video tutorials.

If you decide building a website is more than you want to attempt, you can easily find someone to build one for you at a reasonable price. If both your funds and your knowledge of how to build a website are limited, you can still establish a web presence for just five dollars! Yes, you read that last sentence correctly... $5! How is this possible? On the website www.fiverr.com there are people ready, willing, and able to do a whole variety of things for just $5; including building a website. I've bought a few $5 gigs on this site with great results.

Domain Names

While you're contemplating how to get your website built, you're going to want to decide what name you want to use for your web address. Your 'domain name' is what people will type into an internet browser to find you. The more relevant your website name is to you or your topic of expertise, the easier it will be for your potential customers to find you. Catchy domain names are becoming harder and harder to obtain though, and some of them are quite expensive.

Before 1995, registration of domain names was free and those who were smart enough to see the potential began scooping up the domain names they thought other people would want. Marc Ostrofsky describes in his book *Get Rich CLICK: The Ultimate Guide to Making Money on the Internet* how he was one of those savvy persons who saw the future for websites and secured domain names such as: www.business.com and www.photographer.com.

When I began developing my business many years ago, the first thing I did was to think of all the ways that I wanted my clients to find me. I wanted them to have the option of using my name, the name of my business or phrases that described problems that I could solve for them. Immediately I purchased BillCorbett.com and CooperativeKids.com. In the years since, I've been contacted numerous times by other Bill Corbetts asking me to give up that domain. I've also purchased—and continue to purchase—domains with phrases that represent problems I can solve for my clients, such as: StopTheTantrums.com and ChangeYourKidsBehavior.com.

Start now to think about the names you'd like to have as a web address. You can check to see if they are available simply by going to a domain registrar site and typing the address you'd like to have into their domain search. Two of the more popular domain registry sites are: GoDaddy.com or NameCheap.com. While you're there, take a look at what they offer for website building tools.

You can have more than one domain name assigned to your website. The cost per domain is reasonable; in 2013, around $15. If you want to keep your names beyond the first year you'll have to renew them annually. It's easy to do and your registrar usually sends you a reminder before your year is up. If you don't renew in time, the domain will become available to someone else. Some registrars even offer a waiting service to notify interested parties if you let your domain name expire.

Once you have your domain name and a website ready to go, you'll need a web host. Web hosting is an internet service that puts your website on the World Wide Web so that it is available for viewing by anyone on the internet. There are many options for hosting. Start with your domain registrar first to see if you like what they have to offer. You can also do an internet search for full service web hosting providers; they come with a higher price tag, but they also have a lot of extra tools.

The good thing about websites is that once they are up and running, you have a way for people to find you, even while you're sleeping. Now it's time to focus on what you can do to increase the likelihood of being found.

Getting Found on the Web

There are many ways to get found on the internet. When you're just starting out though, don't worry about figuring out all the ways to do it. It's better to pick a couple of methods and get good at them before moving on to others.

The funny and sometimes frustrating thing about finally getting your website up and running is what happens next, usually nothing. It's a little bit like opening up a new store on a busy street and expecting everyone to beat down the front door to get inside. Your friends and family will all come by and tell you how great it all looks, but they aren't very likely to buy what you're offering.

The nice thing about the web is that it wants to find you, as much as you want it to find you. Web search engines send out 'web crawlers.' Wikipedia explains a web crawler as: "an internet 'bot' that systematically browses the World Wide Web, typically for the purpose of web indexing." Web crawlers are constantly scanning the web for new content to add to its indexes.

When some part of your web content gets found by a web crawler, it gets listed in an index. Once your website or your content is indexed, it will come up in the results of an internet search. The goal is to get indexed as close as you can to the top of those results. The more frequent and diverse your content, the closer to the top of the index it will be. One type of content that both web crawlers and people enjoy is a blog.

Publishing a Blog

If you're not exactly sure what a blog is, that might be because it's used so many different ways. The word blog is actually an abbreviation for 'web log.' A web log consists of a collection of blog posts or blog entries, aka, your content. It's like an electronic version of a journal. The great thing about a blog is that you can use it to talk about anything you want. It can be a personal diary, a way to express your personal opinions, or an invitation to have a discussion with your readers. It can be a running commentary about your less than perfect day job; it can be about current events, articles you've written, what you are doing at the moment, or commentary on what other people are blogging about.

I've used my personal blog to express my thoughts about other parent education experts, outlining why I agree or disagree with their methodology and how my methods compare with theirs. I've also used my blog to promote people or projects that I felt strongly about. When I travel to and from my business events, I usually write a blog post either before I speak or following the event, talking about where I am and describing anything of interest. I've also shared chapters from my book on my blog.

There's not really a limit to what you can use a blog for, but for our purposes here, we are talking about using a blog as a form of social media to increase the likelihood of being found by potential customers, and of course, the web crawlers.

Because blogging is so popular, the web is loaded with resources that can help you set up a blog in a very short amount of time. Two of the more popular blog sites are Blogger.com and Wordpress.com. Each service is free and both provide a plethora of training material to help you get your blog up and running quickly. You can also put your blog on your own website. You don't need a lot of computer experience to have a blog and you don't have to be on the internet to write a blog post. If you want, you can write it from the comfort of your sofa and post it to the internet when it's more convenient.

Your Blog is more likely to be found and read when it's updated frequently. Both readers and the indexing 'bots' love fresh content, and when they like you and what you are blogging about, they will look for your new posts. How often you want to post is a choice you get to make, but once a month is not often enough. Web 2.0 experts suggest posting an update two to three times per week.

One way of getting people interested in your blog is to find, read, and comment on other writer's blogs. Do an internet search on your topic of interest and look through the results to see who else is blogging about your subject. Google even has its own blog search engine to help you narrow your search: www.Google.com/blogsearch.

When you find blogs related to your topic, figure out which ones look like they would have the type of client base you are hoping to build. Most blog posts provide space for reader's comments. If you find a post you agree with, or have something to add, you can post a comment. Chances are good that you will even be able to list your web address as part of your post signature. If readers like your comments, they will be more likely to check out your personal blog to hear what else you have to say.

Some bloggers even invite guest bloggers to post on their site/blog after reading comments they've left. If you don't know the blogger personally then any comments you make will be your informal introduction, so take the time to make sure your posts are relevant and well thought out. Bloggers read the comments their readers leave. If they like your comments, they may ask you to post on their blog. Using this method, I was invited to contribute to a blog that features 31 writers; each writer contributing one blog post on a specific day each month.

Once your blog is up and running, you can also approach people in your topic area to be guest bloggers on your site. They don't even necessarily have to post original content. You could do a 'repost' of one of their past blog posts. Their name recognition helps impress your audience and the new material gives the web crawlers something new to work with.

Facebook

Created by a Harvard University student, Facebook made its internet debut in 2006. Today, it's one of the leading social media sites where people go to communicate, connect, and share. It's also a good place for aspiring entrepreneurs to begin building a following of friends, colleagues, fans, and clients. Creating a Facebook page is free and easy to do; all it requires is having a legitimate email address. If you already have a personal page and are thinking about creating a Facebook business page too, you can do an internet search on 'how to set up a Facebook business page' to get more information.

While Facebook provides a lot of opportunities, there are also things you'll want to keep in mind:

- You need to have a personal Facebook page before you can have a business Facebook page.
- When you post something on any Facebook page, it has the potential of being seen by a lot of people, so don't post things you wouldn't want your business contacts or potential clients to see. Posting is easy; making a post disappear is not.
- Social media works best when it's updated regularly. If you decide to put up a business page, commit to keeping it updated. Old or outdated information reflects poorly on you as a professional.

Linking up with Other Professionals

Web 2.0 networking can be just as advantageous as real world networking. It's always helpful to be able to recognize your fellow professionals and to have them recognize you. Networking provides an equal footing platform where you can interact as professionals and experts within your topic. It can also help build relationships that lead to referrals and recommendations from you, or for you.

One of the leading business oriented social networking sites on the internet is LinkedIn; their website is www.LinkedIn.com. This platform is a sure-fire way of growing your professional network beyond those who already know you. In their words:

"Our mission is simple: connect the world's professionals to make them more productive and successful. When you join LinkedIn, you get access to people, jobs, news, updates, and insights that help you be great at what you do."

Joining LinkedIn and setting up your profile is free. Of course, LinkedIn also offers a premium-level membership with greater capabilities, but starting with the free membership will give you plenty of opportunities to grow your speaking business.

A LinkedIn profile also gives you the opportunity to expand your network by making connections with other professionals interested in networking too. I've heard numerous success stories of professionals establishing connections that resulted in great opportunities and even some amazing job offers. Personally, I've interacted with other professionals looking for information or answers to questions, as well as requests for proposals and estimates that evolved into business opportunities.

If you want to take advantage of all the opportunities LinkedIn has to offer, you'll want to invest some of your time to 'work it.' This means seeking out other professionals to add to your network, posting updates about your current activity, project or trip, and taking time to read the profiles of people already in your network, or profiles of those you're considering asking to join your network.

Another big benefit of LinkedIn is the many discussion groups available to members. Joining a group is a way of meeting and interacting with other like-minded professionals, potential clients, or people you might be able to help in some way. My first search for discussion groups focused on parenting or child behavior topics netted an overwhelming number of groups. If you can't seem to find a group that fits your area of expertise exactly, start your own. I established several of my own discussion groups and instantly, like-minded professionals began joining my group and posting topics or questions for discussion.

Today I get numerous daily requests from other LinkedIn professionals to join their network and in most cases I accept. As soon as I've accepted them as a member of my network, I take a close look at their profile to see if there is a way that I can assist them with their work, or if there is any way they might be able to assist me with mine.

There are many ways of using this great online social networking resource, so I encourage you to log on, set up your free profile, and begin building your network.

Writing Articles to Build Your Content

Articles are everywhere on the internet. They differ from blog posts in that blogs tend to be more conversational whereas articles tend to be more informational. Articles are more diverse than blogs because they can be used in print media as well. Even when you're just getting started as a speaker, writing short 300 – 500 word articles about a topic in your area of expertise, will help build both your confidence and your content. They are also physical proof that you really do know what you're talking about.

Dottie and Lilly Walters highly recommend writing articles. In their book *Speak and Grow Rich* they say:

> One of the best ways to be seen and have your views heard by potential clients is to write and publish articles related to your topic. These articles not only keep you in the public eye, but will keep you in front of buyers in the markets you want to reach as well. While it may be a while before you become an international household name, you can start quickly to be a celebrity expert within your defined market by writing articles for that industry's publications. (Walters & Walters, 1997)

Early in my career as a new speaker, I began writing 300 – 500 word articles by addressing specific questions that parents would ask me. I would attach a cover letter to one of my articles and mail it off to local newspapers to be considered for publication. After several months without any replies, I decided that I needed to narrow the focus of the articles to my area of expertise; parenting. I also started reading the local parenting magazine more thoroughly taking note of the names of both editors and authors.

One day I got an idea. After noticing one particular editor's name frequently attached to articles, I tracked down her email address and sent her an email asking her for some help. I introduced myself as the local parenting expert and asked her if I could buy her lunch in exchange for some guidance from her as the magazine's editor. Amazingly, she agreed and we met at a restaurant she chose. During our lunch, I asked her for some advice on how editors select articles to print. Conveniently, I had also brought along a few samples of some of my best articles to show her.

As a result of that lunch, I landed my first monthly column and two months later my first article appeared in my city's parenting magazine. It was very exciting, but initially I felt the pressure of needing to write a 500 word article every month. I decided to look on this new demand as if I was writing a short college essay every 30 days.

Then something else amazing happened as the result of my picture appearing alongside my monthly column. I started being recognized in the community. This definitely helped me with my objective of building my credibility as an expert in my chosen topic. More and more frequently, someone would approach me and say something like, "Hey, you're the guy that writes the articles about kids and behavior." I would smile and thank them for reading my column.

One woman recognized me while I was in the grocery store and started asking me questions about a problem she was having with her toddler who just happened to be sitting in the cart. It's these moments of recognition and interaction with fans or followers that remind us of how valuable our expertise can be to the people we are sharing it with. We are, whether it's in print, on the internet, over the radio or on TV, in the business of informing others and helping them change or enhance their lives in positive ways.

This strategy can be used by any professional in any industry. Figure out which magazines your customers and potential clients are reading. Look through the articles they are printing and pick a topic you feel confident writing about. After you've written a few articles you're proud of, try contacting the appropriate person and ask them if you can buy them lunch (or coffee) in exchange for some advice on how to get your articles in print. When I took the editor out to lunch, I was hoping for a chance to share my articles, but it would still have been a good meeting even if I'd come away with nothing more than her advice about how to get in print.

Writing articles for the web is another great channel for sharing your knowledge, information, and experience with people who might not have any other access to it. The internet contains a variety of websites looking for experts to submit articles. One of the more popular choices is EzineArticles.com. This website is full of experts who've written articles about their area of expertise. Ezine authors earn 'badges' for completing various actions and achievements based on the quantity and quality of the articles they submit for publication. On their individual author page there is a biography, a summary, a list of badges and awards, and a list of all their articles. It's another tool for building your reputation as an expert.

Whether you decide to write both a blog and articles at the same time, or decide to focus on just one of the two for right now, each is a way to expand your presence and work toward becoming recognized as a knowledgeable professional in your field. With both channels, always stop and take the time to make sure your written words are a reflection of the quality people associate with professionals in general and you in particular.

Double check your grammar and spelling; and if possible, have someone you trust read your blog posts and articles before you publish.

Using Podcasts to Expand Your Reach

A podcast is created by recording the audio portion of your talks, discussions, speeches or commentary, and then making them available for free or for sale on the internet. They are a great way to build your online content. They also solve a problem for people who want to see you in person, or hear you speak, but don't always have the time and opportunity to be at one of your events.

When you create podcasts, you give potential clients another way of learning more about you and what you have to offer. You also give your existing clients a way to access your information whenever they want to hear it.

In technical terms, podcasts are multimedia digital files. In not-so-technical terms they are audio recordings that can be downloaded from the internet and listened to on a computer, laptop, tablet, Smartphone, or MP3 player. The first step in creating a podcast is to make an audio recording using some type of digital recorder. There are excellent personal digital recorders available for under $40 at most electronics stores. You can use them to record your talks, radio interviews, lectures, trainings, discussions with other people, or even to record your thoughts and insights for possible future podcast content. Then, using a USB cable that usually comes with the recorder, you can copy these recorded files onto your computer to edit and then upload them to the internet as podcasts.

Using an iPod or iPhone will work too. In fact, before I bought my pocket-sized digital recorder I used my iPod. I would turn on the voice memo option, lock the device so it wouldn't turn off accidently, and then slip it into my pocket to record anytime I was speaking or working with my clients (with their permission of course). Later, I would upload the voice files from my iPod to my computer and listen to what I had recorded.

There are also many inexpensive audio editors you can download or purchase off the internet. As you get more comfortable with their features, you will be able to increase the quality of your recordings and even do things like adding introductions and follow-up information at the end. At Audacity.com, you can download Audacity, one of the most popular free software programs for recording and editing your clips with ease. A simple internet search will turn up many text and video tutorials on how to use it.

To make your podcast recordings available to the public on a distribution service like iTunes, you'll first have to upload them to a hosting service. This is where they are digitally stored until someone downloads them from a distributor. There are many hosting services out there and a ton of tutorial documents and videos to help you use them. You will pay a subscription fee to have your podcasts hosted; the cost will be relative to the size of the digital storage space you pick.

When it comes to podcasts, you will have greater success if you keep your recordings from 10 – 20 minutes in length. The shorter your recordings are, the more likely people will be to listen to them all the way through. The smaller size also reduces the amount of time needed to upload or download the audio file. A shorter podcast also reduces the amount of digital storage space required on your computer and at the hosting service provider.

Once your podcasts are ready, the easiest way to make them available is to sign up with a service like iTunes. You can see an example of a podcast series on iTunes by viewing mine. Enter the following URL into your internet browser to have a look: http://bit.ly/cckpodcast.

Chapter 9

Speak for Free and Get Noticed

An entrepreneur's business is different from a brick and mortar business; it can't rely on walk-in customer traffic. With a Web 2.0 presence, many of your new and potential clients will be learning more about you or have been referred to you by someone else. Another way to expand your reach is to create your own opportunities for getting noticed by more potential customers. Speaking for free, especially when you are just starting out, is a great way of making connections with people. When they see you in-person, they are more likely to remember you and your content. They may even be the source of your next paying opportunity. The book *Guerrilla Publicity* advises:

> Name recognition isn't simply people knowing who you are; it's also their knowing what you do. They associate your name with your product or service. When you gain name recognition, the public thinks of you when they want your product or service. They will stand in line to do business with you. (Levinson, Frishman, & Lublin, 2002)

Toastmasters

My first official talks or presentations on my topic of expertise were delivered at Toastmasters meetings. As a member of Toastmasters, you have the option of completing a series of assignments that lead to advancing levels of speaking certification. My favorite aspect of this format is that you get to choose the topics you'd like to speak about. In fact, you are encouraged to select topics that you are knowledgeable about to ease the process of developing your speech.

One member of a past chapter sold investment products as

his area of expertise. For the next several months, his speeches were about investments, defining what they were and how to buy the right ones. We learned so much about this topic that some members ended up hiring him or buying his product.

At that time I was still building my content, so many of my initial speeches were focused on parenting related topics. As a result, chapter members came to know me as the local parenting expert. This led to many opportunities for me down the road.

Civic Organizations

Just about every town, city or county has nonprofit organizations such as Kiwanis, Rotary, and Lions Club. These groups are made up of civic-minded professionals who come together with the goal of improving their community or assisting the residents of their community in some fashion. They are also always open to welcoming visiting experts as a way of increasing their general knowledge and learning more about resources the community may benefit from.

These meetings are great places to speak and get noticed in the community because the members have networks both inside and outside of the organization. If your talk resonates with the audience, you might be approached and asked if it's okay to share your contact information with other groups or individuals that could benefit from what you have to say and offer.

My very first talk at a Rotary Club meeting was on the general topic of power struggles with children. Many of the members were parents or grandparents and appreciated the information, but they also asked about my background and knowledge on the topic; many even asked for my business card.

The one thing civic organizations don't usually allow at their meetings is sales presentations or selling your products/services. So when you craft your 20 – 40 minute talk, remember that you are there to share your message. You will make a much better impression when you come across as ready to help, educate, and inform your audience. Go back to my earlier suggestion that when you give a talk in front of a group, instead of providing a speech, provide a solution instead. Think of these free talks as an investment in your future success.

To locate the civic clubs and organizations in your area, look through the meeting notice section of your local newspaper. You can also check the local Chamber of Commerce to see what groups and information are listed there. And, as always, you can search for them on the internet.

Professional Associations

No matter what area of expertise you select, there will be trained professionals who work, guide, mentor, and teach in that field. These professionals usually belong to or subscribe to organized associations that help their members by providing opportunities for continuing education, certification, and information designed to further the efforts and progress of its member.

Investigate which associations your ideal customers belong to. Contact these associations and offer to speak about a topic you believe will be of benefit to their professional members. Join them, subscribe to their publications and seek opportunities to get up in front of them frequently.

In my field of expertise—parenting—the professionals are pediatricians, counselors, therapists, psychologists, and teaching professionals. I did the research to find out which associations they belonged to and contacted those associations to let them know that I would be happy to offer my services in any way that I could. My first efforts resulted in a 20-minute presentation at a luncheon for therapists in my community.

I stayed within the time limit they requested, provided handouts, gave a brief demonstration of my methodology, and handed out business cards when I was done. This free presentation resulted in countless and invaluable referrals to parents who ended up enrolling in my parenting classes.

There are professional associations for just about any interest in the world. If you consider yourself an expert on making children laugh, there may be speaking opportunities with The Association for Applied and Therapeutic Humor. If you are a nurse that works at a children's camp, The Association of Camp Nurses might be very interested in what you have to say. If you've dedicated your life to promoting healthy eating for pets, meetings put on by The Association for Pet Obesity Prevention could be the perfect place for you to get some exposure. The possibilities are endless, regardless of your area of expertise.

If you're still not sure of who to engage, contact professionals in your current network and ask them which professional organizations and associations they belong to or are affiliated with. A therapist I was referring parents to told me about an educational company that conducted webinars (a multimedia seminar broadcast over the internet) as a form of continuing education for therapists.

I contacted the organization to inquire about their seminar services. As a result of the initial contact, I applied for a position as a Webinar Facilitator and was accepted. I conducted a 90-minute webinar on "How to Handle Challenging Children" over the phone while using a PowerPoint I developed on my computer. I did receive a small stipend for this webinar, but it was the professional contacts I made in the process that were far more valuable. Each participant was an ideal client for me, teaching staff and counselors who could potentially hire me down the road. It was an excellent investment that has paid off many times more than the stipend.

Getting Press about Your Talk

Once you've been accepted and are officially listed on someone's calendar as a guest speaker, I recommend using this as an opportunity to get some free publicity by sending a press release to your local media. A press release is an official notification sent to newspapers, radio stations, and TV stations informing them that an event of interest will be taking place in their community.

Most media outlets will publish the details of your upcoming event in their event listings for free. Newspaper editors and other media producers are also always looking for local stories to use as fillers in the local news sections, or as a service to the local community. Getting your name in the news about a presentation you'll be doing will add to your credibility and increase your recognition as an expert and a speaker. And, if your press release results in coverage by one of your local newspapers, you'll have a newsprint item to include in your press/media kit (covered in detail in chapter 14).

How to Write a Press Release

A press release is written in an industry standard format that is easy to follow. Start by making a list of all the Who, What, When, Where, and Whys associated with your talk. Stitch these details into the first paragraph of your press release to give readers the 'nuts and bolts' of your talk right up front. Add additional paragraphs to further describe the event details. Here is an example of a typical press release utilizing the format described above:

FOR IMMEDIATE RELEASE
ANY CITY, MA (09/16/2014)—The ABC School is hosting a lecture on Tuesday, October 5, to provide parents and educators with solutions for keeping children safe on the Internet. The session will be held from 6:00 to 8:00 pm, at The ABC School, 21 Some Such Road, Any City.

Registrations are now being accepted for this interactive session called "Kids and the Internet." This FREE event will provide parents and teachers with easy-to-implement steps for securing your child's experience online.

Internet security expert John Smith, will be the speaker and will take the mystery out of implementing safeguards on social media channels such as Facebook and Twitter for parents and other caregivers. There is no charge to attend this event.

Advance registration is required and a capacity attendance is expected. Call Ms. Smith at The ABC School for more information - (999) 999-9999, or email her at info@abcschool.org to reserve your seat(s). To learn more about the speaker, go to his website at www.InternetSite.com.

Before sending out any press release, make sure to get in touch with your contact at the organization and let that person know you would like to submit a press release about your upcoming presentation to the local media. Because many organizations are interested in getting press as well, they are likely to welcome your idea instantly. Some will even offer to write and send out the press release for you. This is a good scenario because the press release will not be coming from you, the speaker; it will be coming from the organization itself. This scenario also highlights the fact that they are bringing you in to speak to their members as an expert.

Who to Send It To

These days, most press releases are delivered by email, but you'll want to check each local media outlet for their individual preferences. To compile your list of media outlets, start with an internet search of your local community. If you are presenting at a location that is not local to you, be sure to do an internet search for the media outlets there as well. Check out each outlet's website to see if they provide contact information and submission guidelines. If they don't, or you can't seem to find it on their website, you can contact them by phone and ask them for the information directly.

With print media, find the publication's masthead, usually located within the first few pages of the publication itself. This should contain all the contact information you need. Again, if it isn't there, you might have to call. The nice thing about print media is that you can stop at any local convenience store and pick up all the newspapers and any other appropriate publications local to the area and you'll have their information in your hand.

Once you've compiled your list of media email contacts, enter them into your email contacts list. In some ways the email you will be sending out is generic because you're sending everyone the same information; but you'll be sending out your emails to one outlet at a time. Doing it this way gives you the opportunity to develop relationships with the people receiving your press releases. Each one of these emails is another opportunity to present yourself as a business professional as well as an expert in your field.

Once you've written the opening part of your email, you will be pasting your press release into the body. Do not send your press release as an attachment. Thanks to viruses, very few editors or producers accept emails that have attachments.

Editors and producers receive many emails throughout the day and can easily miss what you send. To ensure that your press release email gets noticed, come up with a catchy title for your event. If I were speaking at the ABC school, a catchy title I might use could be: "Parenting Expert Helps Parents Tame the Tantrums." Then, when I send out the email/press release, I would work that title into the subject line to help it stand out.

For more help on writing press releases, there are many books that can teach you all about how to write them. And, as with all the other books I've mentioned throughout this book, you'll be able to find many of them at your local library. You can also do internet searches to find helpful articles and videos on how to construct a great press release.

Finding out when or if your press release is published is not always easy. Some editors might send you a message thanking you for the information and include some idea of when they will try and publish it. Others won't respond at all. I often get confirmation that my press releases were published via emails and phone calls from family and friends letting me know they saw or heard about one of my upcoming events.

Keep in mind that editors and producers are very busy people. If your press release doesn't get printed, don't take it personally. Just keep sending them out anyway because good things can happen. Some of my press releases resulted in coverage by reporters who saw the release and decided to cover the event and write an article about it! You never know what opportunities your press release could create.

It is also acceptable to send out a press release after the fact. This might be necessary if your speaking opportunity came about so quickly you didn't have enough time to get one out. The only difference between a before release and an after release is that it should be written in the past tense, rather than the future. The more press releases you have going out to your local media outlets, the more opportunities you are creating for getting noticed. Just take the time to make sure they are professional and about events that lend credibility to your stature as an expert.

The Thank You Card

Many years ago I found an editorial article written by business and leadership professional speaker, Tom Peters. I was so inspired by his words that I cut out the article and posted it on the wall of my cubicle. His wisdom; when you're running a business, send handwritten thank you notes to the people who help you achieve your goals.

Today, I get to share his wisdom with you. As soon after your event as is possible, sit down and write a brief thank you note to your contact person at the organization that hosted your event. Thank him or her for the opportunity to speak, and invite them to call on you if there is anything you can do to assist them in the future.

With the popularity of email correspondence on the rise, the handwritten thank you note has become a lost art. I can't think of a more genuine way of thanking someone for allowing you to speak to their people. I encourage you to go out and get yourself a box of thank you notes along with a book of stamps to have on hand. If you want, you can even design your own thank you notes. There are many inexpensive online print companies like VistaPrint that will help you design your own unique thank you cards. Professionals who use techniques like this validate their personal professionalism and, in many cases, are invited back or benefit from multiple referrals to other organizations.

The Referral Letter

After you've sent your thank you note and at some point during the following week, I suggest reaching out to your contact with a letter, an email, or a phone call to ask if they would be willing to write you a referral letter. You can explain to them that you will be sharing their written comments with groups thinking about hiring you or inviting you to give talks at one of their events.

Most professionals know the value of having a referral letter and will be happy to provide you with a letter talking about your professionalism and the quality of your presentation written on the company's letterhead stationery. When you're just starting out with your business, it may feel awkward asking for the letter, but this letter will help you get more opportunities in front of other potential client groups. Having written testimonies from past clients is an incredibly powerful way to impress future clients.

If your contact seems hesitant or resistant to the idea of writing a letter, thank them for their consideration and let it go. If they agree to write it but the letter never comes, you can send one more reminder, but after that, just let it go.

Some contacts may be hesitant because they've never written a referral letter and aren't sure what they should say. Explain that it starts with the traditional "To Whom it May Concern." In the body of the letter they can talk about the impact they think your presentation had on their audience. If they're really stuck or they weren't in the room when you spoke, suggest that they reach out to people who were in the audience and ask them for their thoughts about the presentation.

When you do receive referral letters, value them as if they were made out of gold! I suggest keeping the original, along with about 10 – 20 copies, in a folder that you can retrieve easily. You will use the copies to build your media/press kit (chapter 14). The following is a referral letter I received; one of my favorites. I've modified it slightly to fit in this publication and to withhold the identity of my client:

> Tuesday night, we hosted Bill Corbett and 150 parents and professionals at the High School. The response to Bill's presentation was phenomenal. The audience was fully engaged for two hours, made notes, and stayed after for questions. I wanted to share this information and recommend him to you for your own trainings and meetings.
>
> He gives parents simple tools to deal with the tricky issue(s) of discipline (and parental sanity). In my years of teaching and counseling, I've never heard anyone do it better. We arranged for the evening as part of our organization's work in the area of family strengthening and parent outreach.
>
> Our VP for Early Education, said: "I learned of Bill

Corbett through a referral from a very active parent/contributor in our agency. Once I listened/read Bill's work and heard accounts from other parents of his presentation style, I wanted to secure him for part of our work around parent support and education."

It's true that this chapter isn't about making money; it is about making connections. Smart entrepreneurs grow their business by giving free talks whenever they can. They also continue to work at improving and enhancing their content and polishing their presentations so that their message will have the greatest impact on their audience. As you get started, take advantage of the 'free' opportunities to share your message. Good things can come from them when you least expect it.

I once received a call from the director of a local YMCA child care center. My business was new and I was excited that she had heard about me from another source. She was wondering if I would be willing to speak to her teachers about handling young children with challenging behaviors. She was also upfront about the fact that she had no money to pay me and wouldn't blame me if I declined.

I considered the facts involving this opportunity: I was available, I could use the practice presenting, the client was a nonprofit organization helping families, and she was very kind on the call. I decided to accept. On the appointed day, I arrived at the YMCA and delivered my presentation. When I was done, she thanked me and told me how grateful she was that I had agreed to speak even though I wasn't getting paid. Then she surprised me by telling me that she had received a small grant just the day before and presented me with a check for $600. I now had $600 more than I had when I arrived and she had a group of teachers who had received 2 hours of training they needed for their state requirement.

There's a lot to digest in this chapter. To help you out, below is a summary of the information. Listed as action items, they provide an organized plan to get started.

Action Items:

- Develop a few 20-minute talks in your topic that would be of interest to a general audience
- Use the internet to find your local Toastmasters club and join
- If you're already a member, seek out opportunities at other Toastmasters clubs in your area
- Check your local newspapers for Kiwanis, Rotary, and Lions Club meeting notices
- Call the Chamber of Commerce in your area to find other local civic groups/organizations
- Call their chapter presidents and offer to speak at one of their meetings
- Use the internet or your library to find groups organized around your topic of interest
- When you find these groups or organizations, find out if they have a local presence and join
- Attend local events put on by groups/organizations that share an interest in your topic area
- Begin building a contact database of your local newspaper editors and radio/TV producers
- If you don't already have an email box or want to set up a separate email address for your speaking business, you can go to Yahoo, Google, or Hotmail and open one
- Check with your website hosting service; they may offer email accounts at little or no charge
- Go to a stationary store and buy a box of thank you cards and a book of stamps, or go to www.VistaPrint.com and design your own
- Prepare a small stack of file folders and have them ready to hold your referral letters
- Get yourself out there and speak for free!

CHAPTER 10

Getting Noticed in Print and on the Radio

Print Media

The interesting thing about your name and your work appearing in the newspaper is that you never know who's going to see it and then be inspired to do some Web 2.0 surfing to find out more about you. The more opportunities you give them to see your name and learn about you and what you do, the more likely they are to recognize you as the kind of professional they want to do business with.

The good thing about press releases is that they aren't just for announcing events. You can and should use them to let people know about other aspects of your professional life including your accomplishments and achievements. Sending out a press release is a great way to let people know you've written a book, received an award, achieved some milestone, or were promoted within your own organization. Each release is also more evidence of your professional status.

When you decide to submit a press release, always make sure it's formatted correctly. Check out the notices that are currently listed in the publications you are sending your releases to. They are examples of what the publisher will print and how it might look after it's published. If you still have questions about how to write it, do an internet search to find examples of press releases for your specific situation. Always double check for grammar and typos. It's also a good idea to have someone else read it before submitting.

Another advantage to press releases is that people seeing your name over and over might decide to contact you directly. It could be a reporter who's decided to write an article about you;

it could be a potential client. Make it easy for them to contact you by making sure your release contains enough information about how to get in touch with you or your contact person.

While most press releases can be submitted via email, there are still publishers who ask for them to be faxed. The good news is that you don't need a physical fax machine to fax your press release. There are many online fax services that are incredibly affordable. You upload your document to their site, enter the fax phone number, and they send it directly to the publisher for you.

To make sure your press releases are always going to the right place or person, keep your publishing/media contact information updated. Every few months, put aside some time to check their websites and mastheads to make sure the contact information and submission guidelines you have are still valid.

Opportunities with Talk Radio

Talk radio is another great avenue for getting exposure. Most radio stations have a website these days, and you can go there to check out their local programming for shows that might be a good fit for your topic. Once identified, you can start submitting your press releases to that show's producer(s) or host(s).

One thing about radio though, some shows will charge you a fee to be a guest. The reason for this is that many small, non-syndicated, AM talk show radio hosts have to pay a fee to their radio station to do their show. They in turn charge their guests a fee to help offset their costs. They also get sponsors for their shows as another way to help defray the costs. Hosts and producers who have been on the air for a long time have learned how to work with this set-up and use it to earn significant income.

My radio show started shortly after being introduced to a woman who hosted a regular weekend talk radio show focused on health and wellness topics. She invited me to be the primary guest on her show as an expert in parenting. The fee she requested was reasonable, so I accepted the offer. Throughout the show she announced the name of my website and told listeners they could also go to her website to get my information. The show brought in so many calls from parents looking for help with their parenting issues, that the station manager offered me a weekend time slot to do my own show; for a nominal fee, of course. Within just a few short weeks, I found myself on the air with a microphone in front of me.

I called my radio show "The Parent Talk Show" and it was broadcast on a local 15,000 watt radio station. I had never hosted a radio show before, so I listened and learned from other shows. I even managed to get a few sponsors to help pay my hosting bill. Within a few months, my show information had made its way onto internet lists of radio talk shows. Entrepreneurs from around the country started hearing about my show and decided they wanted to be a featured guest. That's when the calls and merchandise began rolling in! I continued sending out press releases to local media and was gaining new listeners weekly.

Then something amazing happened. An executive from Clear Channel, the largest mogul in the radio business, saw one of my press releases and called me! He invited me to a meeting at their corporate office and made me an offer to move my show over to the Clear Channel network. At that point in time, Clear Channel owned the top rock, country, rap, pop, and talk radio stations in the city. They were interested in attracting more families to their networks and felt that including my show in the lineup was just what they needed on their 50,000 watt talk radio network.

With a larger listening audience and a real engineer talking to me through my headset on the other side of the glass, I couldn't contain all the ideas that started bursting through my brain. The first thing I did was invite a friend who was also knowledgeable on the topic of parenting to join me on my show as my co-host. Patricia had the 'gift of gab' and complimented me on the air tremendously. With our dialogue and humor, and a full line up of in-studio and on-the-phone guests, our listener base continued to grow. It didn't take long before we began receiving special invitations and free tickets to family-related events. People also started to recognize us outside the studio.

This amazing experience gave me countless opportunities to increase my status as the city's 'go to guy' on the topic of parenting. It also gave me the opportunity to interview a variety of experts, authors, doctors, and others known for their work with families, children, and parenting. I've seen other radio talk show hosts succeed with topics they were experts in: money, investments, law, automobiles, etc. Becoming a radio talk show host is just another great option for those who want to expand their business.

Internet Radio

The big difference between now and when I had my radio show is the increasing popularity of Internet radio. Websites like BlogTalkRadio.com and WebTalkRadio.com allow anyone with an internet connection and some creativity to create their own internet talk radio show. If having your own radio show has always been one of your dreams, now is the time to jump on board; it's never been easier. If you're still not sure this is a good option for you, find existing internet radio talk shows and give them a listen. At the very least, you might find a few shows you could contact about the possibility of being an expert guest.

Another great benefit of internet radio shows is that recordings of your completed shows and interviews will make great additions to your podcasts. Even if you don't have your own show, seek out opportunities to be a guest on other shows and then ask the show's host or producer for the link to your interview once it's edited and ready. You can then download the recording, further edit it by adding your own recorded header and footer, and then upload it as another episode in your podcast collection.

Chapter 11

Getting on Television

Major network affiliate channels such as: ABC, NBC, CBS, FOX, etc., offer great opportunities for both free and paid exposure for you and your business. The producers of local news and magazine shows are always looking for local experts to appear on air for interviews related to topics of interest to their viewers. Appearing on television can be one of the quickest ways to become known as the local 'go to' expert.

Television producers are constantly scrambling to create news worthy content, and getting on their list of people they know they can call for up-to-date and informative commentary on timely topics when needed is likely to result in multiple invitations to appear on camera. I've been called many times and asked if I would be willing to come in and be interviewed about various parenting issues. Sadly, not all on camera visits are happy ones.

On the morning of December 14, 2012, 20 first graders and 6 staff lost their lives at Sandy Hook Elementary School in Newtown, Connecticut. The news story broke late that morning and all of Connecticut, as well as the rest of the country, was devastated by the news of this tragic shooting. Even today, people across our planet continue to struggle with the reality of what happened.

Around 2 p.m. that day, my office phone rang and it was the producer from an ABC affiliate I had worked with many times. They were preparing for a special report at 5 p.m. and needed a parenting expert to provide some guidance for parents on how to help their children cope with the tragedy. I agreed and within an hour I was on the road.

When I arrived, I was ushered into the studio and prepped for the news. I was seated on the set next to the popular 5 p.m.

news anchors. They briefed me on the questions they were going to ask and then I was interviewed on camera for nearly the entire 30 minute news program.

Personally I can tell you that the one hour drive to the ABC studios was incredibly difficult. Like everyone else, I was still in a state of shock over what had happened. But I also felt honored at having been the person the producers thought to call at a moment's notice. I was also incredibly grateful for the opportunity to be able to help by sharing information, ideas, and strategies with parents and caregivers who would then be able to better help their children deal with what happened.

How to Become the 'Go To' Person TV Producers Call

Start by making a list of all the major network affiliates in your area. If you're not sure who they are, look through a TV programming guide. Local Sunday newspapers usually include a TV guide supplement that will list all the stations in your area. You can do an internet search to determine where their physical studios are located and decide which ones you would be willing to drive to at a moment's notice. Begin watching the shows you think you might like to appear on and familiarize yourself with the names of the on-air talent hosting the local news, information, and style programs.

If the names and contact information for the producers aren't on the affiliate's website, you can always call the stations directly. Then, call or email the producers with a brief outline of your biographical information, a list of topics you're prepared to speak on, and contact information. Offer to send them a resume or CV (Curriculum Vitae) outlining your expertise.

Wherever I've lived, I've always made connections with the producers of the local news programming on the major affiliate stations. I also send them regular brief emails with topic suggestions. If I hear about a breaking news story that has a family/child/parenting angle, I might send the producers a quick email describing how I could help them with information, ideas, strategies, and/or commentary.

As a 'go to' on-camera contributor to most of the major affiliate networks in the cities where I've lived, I've also been asked to come in at some pretty inconvenient times of day. I once was called in at 4 a.m. to offer advice to parents on how to keep their kids safe after a news story broke about a child being abducted while waiting for a school bus.

By demonstrating a willingness to go into their studios at just about any hour and provide them with the professional expertise they're looking for, you too, can become one of their 'go to' people. One thing you'll want to know about being asked to appear on these shows though; they don't pay money. The compensation for being an on-camera contributor comes from your enhanced recognition factor and how much it adds to your credibility as an expert.

I also want to offer a few words of advice on working with print, radio or television media. To obtain the greatest level of success working with them, you must use your highest level of patience. Remember that news media professionals work in high pressure environments with extremely tight deadlines. They are not obligated to fulfill the requests of the general public and this means that you will rarely get replies to your queries, they won't always print your press releases, and they could postpone or cancel a scheduled appearance with little or no notice.

There have been numerous occasions when I drove quite a distance to appear on a local affiliate news program, was seated, briefed, and wired with a microphone, only to be suddenly told the segment was preempted by a breaking news story. If you want to stay on your media contacts good side, be kind, be patient, and be forgiving. And, no matter what, be available, be polite, be professional, and be ready to go when and wherever they need you.

Using Community Access TV to Increase Your Influence

If you really want to take your expertise and your message to the television airwaves with more creative control, consider developing your own television show using public access TV. Many U.S. and international towns and cities have public or community access television stations and studios that are provided for the sole purpose of allowing its residents to create their own programs.

There are several different types of community access TV stations. One type you might be familiar with is owned and maintained by the municipal town or city government and used primarily for broadcasting official meetings or municipal business events. They don't always have an actual TV studio, but have equipment that can be used at your location and a small staff to provide training on how to use it.

Another common type of community access TV is provided by the local cable television conglomerate. Through agreements with local government, these large cable networks sometimes provide very elaborate and plush studios that any resident of the community can use to produce their own TV show. The studio coordinator will train you and help you find and coordinate staff to run state of the art video and broadcasting equipment. All it takes is a crew of trained people and some creativity to create a unique and interesting local television show.

I was lucky enough to find one of those elaborate and plush studios at our local cable offices. As soon as I saw it I decided to take advantage of this opportunity and design a parenting show with a format and style similar to that of mainstream talk shows, minus all the soap opera-like drama. I wanted the show to have segments because even when they're interested, most viewers have been trained by network TV to expect frequent breaks.

I decided that my show would be one hour in length; with five 9-minute segments separated by commercial breaks. Because I was the show's producer, it was my job to develop topics, find guests to interview, organize and write my content, and put together a crew to work the equipment.

As of the publication of this book, my crew and I are entering our fourth year in production with my parenting show called *Creating Cooperative Kids*. We tape one show per month, and thanks to free distribution websites like Pegmedia.org and Telvue.com, my show is currently airing on community access channels in over 250 communities worldwide.

The one thing you'll want to know about community access television is that its goal is to educate and inform; it's not to provide another stage for commercial programming. This means that you cannot use the show to promote your business or to openly sell your products or services on camera. But, if your show educates and entertains the community, and is visually appealing, your viewers will become familiar with you and know exactly how you can help others. I receive emails all the time from people who saw my TV show and then searched for me on the internet.

If working with 2.0 strategies is still new to you, please don't get overwhelmed with the thought that you have to add becoming a radio and TV star to your to-do list. You don't. Ideas like these are simply suggestions of ways to stand out and above your competitors. The good news is that when you are ready, the information will still be here to remind you of the steps you can take to expand your career even further. You'll be reminded of what kinds of opportunities to look for, and how to take advantage of them when they show up on your doorstep. Using them will help you stand out even more as an expert and as a professional.

Action Items:

- Make a list of all the major TV network affiliates in your area

- Use internet or library resources to determine where their studios are located and which ones you would be willing to drive to at a moment's notice
- Begin watching each of your affiliate networks as often as you can to familiarize yourself with the local programming and the names of the anchors hosting them
- Call those news stations and ask the receptionist for the names and contact information for the producers of the programming you are interested in
- Call or email those producers to provide them with your biographical information, topics you're prepared to speak on, and how they can get in touch with you

Chapter 12

Conducting Public Seminars

There was a notice in the newspaper that caught my attention one day. The headline read "How to Live Happier and Get Further Ahead at Work." That headline spoke to me because it stated exactly what I wanted. I immediately read the first paragraph and learned that a 90 minute lecture was being held at 6 p.m. that night at the local Holiday Inn. The cost was just $35 to attend. I thought to myself "Thirty five dollars is a pretty cheap price to pay for learning the secret of how to live a happier life." I showed the ad to a friend and he agreed to go with me.

This was right around the same time I was starting my new business so I wasn't just interested in the content of the lecture, I was also curious about how the expert had put it together. This speaker/expert was going to be talking about something I was very interested in, it was open to the public, and he was getting paid to do it.

My friend and I showed up a few minutes before 6 p.m. and were surprised by the line of people waiting to get inside the hotel conference room. My first reaction was "Wow, whoever this speaker is, he already seems to have accomplished his goal." Of course I didn't really know what his goal was, but I counted at least 20 people ahead of me and 20 people at $35 a head would have made the newbie in me very happy. Now, I was even more invested in hearing the content of the lecture and learning more about how to organize a public lecture.

As I entered the room, I was greeted by a young lady sitting at a table. She had a cash box and was collecting the $35 registration fee from everyone who entered. When I looked into the room I noticed a middle-aged man setting up a flip chart at the front of the room. My first thought was that he was probably the speaker, but what really caught my attention was the rows of chairs filled with people all watching the man setting up the flip chart. There were over 30 people in the room and there were still people in line behind me.

Instantly, I started doing calculations in my head; 35 people times $35 was over $1200! I was impressed and thinking to myself "This guy is going to make over $1200 telling us how to live a happier life." Being curious, I turned to the woman on my left and introduced myself. I asked her how she heard about this lecture. She said that her friend had gotten a flyer at work and asked her if she wanted to come with her. After hearing what she said, another question entered my mind: how did he distribute the flyers? I also wanted to get a look at that flyer and find out where else he had passed them out.

The clock on the wall showed the time was straight up 6 p.m. and the man moved to the front of the room and introduced himself. He rattled off his credentials, mentioning his college degree and where he had spoken before. None of those things meant a whole lot to me at the time, but he had my attention. He then asked us all to think of the worst problem we were dealing with at work and to share the problem with the person next to us. If we didn't have a problem at work, he said to think of one we were experiencing in our personal life that would be appropriate to share with someone.

For the next few minutes the room got quite loud while everyone in the audience was sharing their worst problem at work, at home, or with life in general. The speaker stood quietly at the front of the room observing. After a few minutes, he regained our attention, opened a huge plastic bag, and began handing out golf ball sized, red, foam balls.

Once everyone had a ball in their hand, he brought our attention to the fact that each ball had a slight split in it. He instructed us to gently open the split using our thumbs and then to place the ball on our nose. I thought it was kind of strange, but when I looked around the room, everyone was wearing a red clown nose. Laughter broke out in the room and for a little while, the speaker had no control over his audience. When he was ready to get our attention again, he calmly raised his hand and when the room had quieted, he instructed us to keep our noses on and turn back to our neighbor so we could continue talking about our worst problem.

Once again, laughter broke out and the room was filled with everyone talking and laughing hysterically. We were all looking at our neighbor, listening to them describing their worst problem while wearing a red clown nose. Again, after a few minutes the speaker regained our attention and asked us if we felt any different about our problem after describing it this time. Everyone said or nodded yes. He pointed out that all it took to change our disposition and perspective of our problem was a silly little clown nose.

I was impressed! This was an excellent example of using humor and laughter as a strategy for creating a memorable moment at the beginning of a presentation. By engaging our emotions at the beginning of his talk, this speaker had earned our undivided attention and increased his chances of keeping our attention for the rest of the talk.

The next 90 minutes went by incredibly fast and before I knew it, the speaker was wrapping up his talk. As part of his conclusion, he announced that he would be conducting a longer, half-day session for those who wanted more of what he had to offer. If I remember correctly, he was offering the extended session for $65 and invited us to sign up that night to take advantage of the special offer. I wasn't interested in the extended session, but many people were and I was amazed at the number of them lining up to register for it.

I learned a lot from this speaker. He obviously had a good plan; create some valuable content, find a location, publicize the event, show up, and conduct a top-notch presentation. But there was more. He also created an 'up-sell' opportunity for himself by providing his audience with an additional opportunity to hear and learn more. It's also possible that he had more products to offer at the end of the half-day seminar such as: a full day seminar or a personal coaching program.

After attending several public seminars, I felt like I had a good understanding of how they were put together and decided to give it a try on my own. One of the strategies I used when I started developing a plan for my first public seminar was Stephen R. Covey's 2nd habit in his book *The 7 Habits of Highly Effective People*, "begin with the end in mind." In his book he says:

> To begin with the end in mind means to start with a clear understanding of your destination. It means to know where you're going so that you better understand where you are now and so that the steps you take are always in the right direction. (Covey, 1989)

Although Mr. Covey was talking about creating an ultimate vision for your life, I was using it as a strategy for planning a product. As a behavior expert, I wanted to design a parenting class that would take place over three weekends and cost $99. The class would teach parents how to get more cooperation from their children by changing the way they disciplined them. I used Covey's "begin with the end in mind" strategy, along with the methodology the Holiday Inn speaker had used, as a 1-2-3 blueprint for developing my own idea.

Step one was to figure out how much information to share during the initial public seminar. I had really liked the way the Holiday Inn speaker had used humor to minimize how we felt about the problems in our lives. So, one of my objectives was to create a fun, 90 minute presentation filled with helpful advice that my participants could begin to use immediately, regardless of whether they decided to sign up for my 3 week class or not. My hope was that people would feel so good about the quality of information, ideas, and strategies that I had shared with them so far, that they would be inspired to sign up for more.

Step two was to find a location to hold this 90-minute introductory lecture. I examined my network and contacted everyone I knew who had access to a facility. I could have gone the route of renting a hotel conference room, but my end-in-mind vision was for a much larger crowd.

One of my contacts was the director of a church preschool who agreed to let me use the church's fellowship hall. Because she needed training hours for her teachers, we worked out a deal that allowed me to use the hall for free if her teachers could attend for free. It was a perfect win-win scenario.

Step three was creating the publicity that would bring people to my event. I created a flyer that I wanted to get into the hands of every parent who brought their child to a day care facility located within a 25-mile radius of the church. I engaged a friend of mine who had desktop publishing skills and together we created an attractive and professional looking flyer. I dropped off copies of the flyer to about a dozen of the largest schools in the surrounding area.

To get print media publicity, I submitted a press release to the three major newspapers that parents in the area were likely to read. I also wanted to see if I could get a reporter to cover the event, so I went to one of the newspaper offices and was able to speak with one of the reporters directly. I gave her a copy of both the press release and the flyer, explained who I was, and gave her the details of what I would be offering at the event. She told me that someone would be in touch if they decided to do a story on my lecture.

The night of my event arrived and I showed up an hour early to set up my equipment. I had prepared a PowerPoint presentation and an accompanying lecture along with some demonstrations. As the flyers and press releases had announced, the ticket price was $12. My registration table was situated right next to the front door, just like at the Holiday Inn, and managed by someone from the church preschool.

I had no idea how many people would actually show up, so I crossed my fingers and waited to see what would happen. The event was scheduled to start at 6:00 p.m.; the first attendees arrived around 5:30 p.m. To my surprise, a young woman approached me and introduced herself as a reporter from the newspaper office I had gone to. She interviewed me and said she was going to stay for a while but might have to leave early. It did not escape my attention that she stayed for the entire evening!

By the time 6:00 p.m. rolled around, over 80 people had walked through the door and paid their $12 to attend my event. At the end of my presentation, I announced the details of my special 3-week class, including the fact that there were a limited number of seats available. About 15 people got in line to register and pay their deposit to be in the special class. My take for the night? Close to $1500 in cash and checks. A week later, the newspaper ran a full page article – with pictures – on the event. It also included information about my 3-week parenting class!

Again, no one expects you to go out and immediately start offering public seminars when you're just getting started as an expert in your field. These two events though, the Holiday Inn talk and my public seminar, are good examples of a formula for using a brief, information packed, one-evening public seminar as a way of inspiring potential clients to sign up for higher-end products such as: training, classes, coaching, consulting, etc. It's also another way to increase your recognition as the 'go to' expert within your topic.

Another way to use this formula is to set up everything online. It isn't necessarily a better way to do it; it's just different. Both situations are focused around an initial presentation with a products or services offer at the end. The one big difference between the two set-ups is that the online presentation is probably free to attendees. Another advantage to an online approach is that you can offer many of your products in a digital format. This means no physical objects to deal with: no stamps, and no shipping cost.

Some people like the online approach because it doesn't feel quite as scary as getting on a stage in the real world. If you enjoy working on your computer, the online formula might be a good option for you. But even online, where you can deliver your content with the push of a button, you still need to be delivering quality content for both the initial offering and with the products and services offered at the end. Take the time to build quality online content and you will be able to make money while you sleep. In his book *KaChing: How to Run an Online Business that Pays and Pays*, author Joel Comm writes:

> Books – both digital and traditional, DVDs, webinars, and online courses are just some of the ways that you can create information products. Online entrepreneurs are using these methods, and I have successfully used many of these methods, too. But it's not the format that's important. It's always the information. (Comm, 2010)

The public seminars I described earlier in this chapter took place before the internet and social media options were mainstream phenomena. Today, there are still plenty of speakers offering public seminars and events, but the number of entrepreneurs learning and mastering the art of delivering their message online is growing. The online advantages are just too good to pass up and they're likely to get better as 2.0 tools and strategies become more flexible, popular and available.

An online event starts with a website that provides information about an upcoming webinar as well as a way to register for it. Instead of press releases, speakers use multiple social media channels along with their email lists to get the word out and invite people to attend their informational/educational webinar.

Interested parties go to the website, register online, and receive an email confirmation with details of when and how to log onto the webinar. When it's time, the presenter(s) begin their virtual, information-packed presentation, delivered directly to your computer, from theirs, via the web.

At the conclusion of the webinar, participants are welcome to log off and go about their day, or to consider purchasing the additional opportunities that were offered towards the end of the webinar. Those products and services might be delivered in a variety of formats including: more webinars, DVDs, coaching calls, or classes delivered by email. Some offers combine a variety of formats to accommodate a variety of customer preferences.

When I was writing this chapter, I went in search of books and websites that offered step-by-step instructions for setting up an online system of seminars/webinars as a way to invite the public to hear your message. What I found was a lot of different ideas. That's one of the challenges with the internet; there are so many ways to do something that sometimes it's hard to figure out where and how to start.

My suggestion is to sign up and attend a few webinars. Start a list of what you liked and didn't like about them. Ask yourself what you would do different. Ask people in your network if they ever attend or use webinars. If they do, pick their brains for information and their list of what they like and don't like.

Although some say that it's becoming more and more difficult to fill chairs with the old style 'Holiday Inn public seminar,' it can still be a viable option when you can offer great content to the right audience. I've used this 1-2-3 plan many times; sometimes pulling in small audiences, other times packing the room to standing-room-only capacity.

As an entrepreneur, you want to have several options for getting your content noticed. The great thing about seminars and webinars is that they very often share the same content. The logistics may be different, but when it comes to outlining and developing the content, you should be able to present it in either scenario without having to make too many alterations.

Chapter 13

Speaking at Professional Conferences

Professional conferences are great marketing opportunities for experts ready to speak or conduct training in front of an audience. When you find a conference organized around your topic, it's safe to say that your audience will be full of potential clients and possible referral sources. They like what you have to offer, and then share the information about your products and services with their network of contacts and clients.

Conferences come in all forms but are primarily designed to bring together a group of people with a shared interest. People attending conferences look forward to the opportunity to network, attend educational seminars, visit vendor displays, and attend any association meetings that might have been scheduled.

Conferences are platforms that encourage and promote organizational development and will vary in size. A local conference may only have 100 people in attendance while a regional conference might have several thousand. There are state conferences, regional conferences, national conferences, and even international conferences.

To find out what kinds of conferences you should be looking at, connect with professionals who are also potential or ideal clients and ask them what conferences they attend. As your relationships with other professionals progress, they may even be willing to help you get connected with a conference planning committee.

I know someone who considers himself a fitness and health expert. He developed a unique style of exercise that he combined with a specific healthy eating plan. He started his speaking business by using his knowledge and expertise in his area to create a few talks he could deliver with little or no preparation. He began speaking for free and within two years, he was speaking at conferences.

A woman I met was an avid gardener and had one of the best looking gardens in the city. She decided she wanted to speak about gardening, so she could share her knowledge, passion, and expertise. She sought out the American Horticultural Association and eventually spoke at an annual horticultural association symposium.

If you're not sure if you should speak at conferences or not, I'll tell you right now, you should. When you start looking at conferences to see what kinds of speakers they are looking for, you will notice that there are usually two types of speakers: the featured keynote speaker and the general workshop speaker. This chapter will focus on how to find and take advantage of opportunities to be a general workshop speaker. Keynote speakers will be covered in chapter 20.

How Conferences Find Speakers

To find their speakers, conference planning committees usually publish what's called an RFP which stands for: Request for Proposals. RFP's can usually be found on the website or in other association publications such as: newsletters, magazines, emails, etc. The timing for RPFs varies greatly and can be announced anywhere between three months to a year or more before the conference date. Each conference committee tells you how they want your proposal submitted. Some committees provide their own web-form with instructions; others give guidelines for a proposal you write and then submit. Make sure to look for the deadline so that you can submit your proposal well in advance of that date.

Some conferences require candidates submitting proposals to be members of the association before they can be considered; some don't. It's always a good idea to support one or more of the associations within your field of expertise by becoming a member. By joining, in addition to supporting the association/organization, you will also have access to all kinds of benefits including: being notified of upcoming conferences and other events, opportunities for increasing your own knowledge base within your field of interest, and the opportunity to network with the 'movers and shakers' within the association.

Being selected as the conference keynote is the ultimate goal of a lot of speakers, but until you reach that level of recognition and are comfortably established as one of the leading experts in your field, being a workshop speaker is a great way to start establishing yourself.

The benefits are excellent when you're a new speaker. Although some conferences pay workshop speakers to facilitate a workshop, the greater benefit is being seen and heard by members of the association, aka, your audience of ideal clients. In these workshops you will have the opportunity to showcase your extensive knowledge as an expert and as a speaker. In fact, some conferences don't call them workshops; they call them a 'Speaker's Showcase.'

Conference committees pay their workshop speakers anywhere between nothing and a few hundred dollars. And because the association putting on the conference is often a nonprofit organization, some of them will even give their workshop speakers the opportunity to donate their small honorarium back to the organization as a donation.

Needless to say, workshop speakers don't get rich. But if the conference offers a stipend, it might cover a majority of your expenses. Either way, it's not the money that's center stage here; it's the exposure you get from being able to showcase your amazing knowledge and skills.

Each person attending your workshop is a potential client who might enjoy your presentation so much that they'll want to hire you for future work. Hearing people say "Great presentation!" as they are leaving is good, but nothing is sweeter than your participants waiting for you after the workshop and asking, "Do you have a business card?" and "Are you available to do this presentation for others?"

The process of becoming a keynote speaker may be a little different, but it starts with meeting planners and coordinators finding out how good you were as a workshop presenter. In most cases when I was selected as the conference keynote speaker, I received the opportunity after receiving rave reviews from people attending my conference workshops. Those evaluations were read by the conference committee, and I was invited to submit a keynote proposal for the following year.

Tips for Being a Welcome Addition to Every Conference

Conference committees change every year, but the core group of members tends to stay the same. What this means to you is that you will be remembered; how they will remember you, is your choice. To be remembered well, know what's expected of you. Be aware of the rules and try to follow them because if you violate them, the committee may forgive, but they won't forget.

If this is the first time you will be submitting to a specific conference, then the first impression you make will be with your proposal. To make a good first impression, follow their detailed instructions as you prepare your proposal and double check it before you submit.

Once you have been selected and scheduled as one of their workshop speakers, follow their rules for presenters. Like the civic groups and organizations, conferences don't approve of their workshop speakers selling their products from the stage. Again though, you're there to share your knowledge and expertise. You'll have plenty of opportunities to talk about what you have to offer as soon as you step off the stage.

Most conferences provide speakers with the option of acquiring a vendor table. Depending on the conference, the table could be free, at a reduced rate, or at the regular price. If you want the opportunity to openly sell your products and services directly to conference attendees, securing a vendor table is your best option. Having a table also lets the committee know that you have a clear understanding of the distinction between presenting a non-sales lecture or workshop, and a workshop that tries to sell to the audience.

Sometimes you can legitimately refer to your products and services without it sounding or looking like a commercial. To bring my audience's attention to my book, I might read an excerpt from it that pertains directly to the subject I'm speaking about.

Sometimes it's a fine line though, and it will most likely be drawn by the audience you are presenting to. If they feel like you were trying to sell them something rather than offering a solution or your expertise, the committee will read about it in your evaluations. The simple result will be that any future proposal from you will be turned down.

At conferences where it's allowed, I usually hold a drawing to give away copies of my books, CDs, or other products at the end of my lecture. I ask my participants to write their name and email address on the entry blanks, but tell them that including their email address is optional. The email addresses I get from my audience are then added to an email list that I use to keep audiences connected to me and my work through newsletters and informative emails long after my presentation has ended.

As with any business, being on time and staying within your allotted time is very important. Arrive at your lecture room early enough to quickly test any technical equipment and/or electrical connections you might be using. I once attended a workshop session on "Technical Presentations in the Digital Age." The presenter arrived when the workshop was supposed to begin and spent the next 30 minutes wrestling with the equipment. By the time she got everything to work, she had about 20 minutes to complete her presentation before people started walking out.

I couldn't help but wonder how her audience had rated her presentation.

Make sure your talk fits precisely within the time frame you've been given. Finishing much earlier than your allotted time could be a problem for conferences that are providing required training hours for its participants.

Going over your allotted time is just as bad because you'll lose your audience's attention as soon as you start going over. At that point they aren't listening to you; they're thinking about the break they should be enjoying. Going over your allotted time is also disrespectful to the speaker who might be following you. They are professionals too and need time to set up and prepare for their presentation just like you.

Make the most of your time off the stage by networking. You'll want to collect as many business cards as you can to begin building your professional network. Be sure to visit the vendor tables to learn more about the products and services being offered. Take the time to write down any ideas that pop into your mind rather than trying to remember them. They might turn into future products or services of your own down the road.

In general, the rules you associate with presenting yourself as a professional outside of a conference apply inside the conference as well. Dress appropriately and professionally. After the conference, make sure to send thank you notes to the organizers and anyone else you'd like to thank for their help.

Now that you know what the rules of the game are, go find your conferences and let your lectures begin!

Preliminary Action Items:

- Continue to build your list of organizations interested in your area of expertise
- Ask people in your professional and personal networks what organizations and associations they belong to

- Find their conference/organization/association websites and become a member if it is appropriate to do so
- Set up calendar reminders to check conference listing information regularly
- Read the instructions for submitting RFPs, write, and then submit your proposals
- Develop your conference presentations and practice them to ensure that they fit within the allotted time
- Ask a colleague to video tape your presentation and watch it with someone who can coach you
- Attend other local organization's conferences to get familiar with what conferences are like
- Seek out others who have spoken at conferences and ask them to mentor you

Once You Are Invited to Speak at a Conference:

- Remember that the value of speaking at a conference outweighs your costs
- Collect your audience's email addresses through a drawing and enter them into a database
- 'Work' the vendor area at conferences to get to know the people and invite them to know you
- Swap business cards with other presenters and vendors, and connect with them on LinkedIn
- Donate items to the conference raffle
- Donate your conference honorarium back if you can afford to do so
- Follow up with a handwritten thank you note to the conference organizers
- Within a week following the conference, ask the organizers for a referral letter
- Recommend other good speakers to conference planners, they will love the help
- Read your evaluations with an open mind

- Show the evaluation comments to a mentor and ask for suggestions or coaching
- Add your conference experience to your online resume on LinkedIn
- Add your conference experience to your resume or CV

Chapter 14

Building Your Marketing/Press Kit

It's really great when meeting planners, event coordinators or potential clients reach out to you for more information about you, your work, and your services. Now that your business is starting to take off, you will also have more articles in print, testimonials, references, etc. to share with them as evidence that you are professional. That's a good thing because it's not always easy to have a conversation about your accomplishments and how great you are without sounding like an advertisement for yourself. It might also be the case that your initial conversation is with someone organizing a pool of potential speaker candidates rather than with the person in charge of choosing the speaker.

This is where a marketing/press kit (MPK) comes in handy. It is a collection of items that provides information about you, your skills, accomplishments, a list of topics you are able to speak about or provide training for, references, and anything else that pertains to your status as an expert, all conveniently collected and delivered in one glossy folder. These kits are physically put together ahead of time so that they are on hand to mail or deliver in person. You can also build an MPK digitally on your computer and save it as a PDF that can be sent by email. You can even upload the components of your MPK to your website. If you'd like to see an online MPK, I invite you to go to my website, www.BillCorbett.com, and click on the Press/Media tab to check out mine. Having all these versions available gives people interested in learning more about you, a choice of how they'd like to receive the information.

Below is a list of the items used to build an MPK followed by an explanation of what each item is. Because you're just starting out, your MPK may be thin. That's okay, we all start somewhere. The goal is to start collecting now, so you can start building your MPK. As your collection grows, you can even begin to organize items into MPKs designed for specific audiences. You can also use recent additions to replace old or outdated items. Keeping your MPK updated shows that you're not just a professional, you're also an *active* professional.

Marketing/Press Kit Inventory:

- Speaker's one-sheet
- CV
- Letters of recommendation
- Newspaper/Magazine/Journal articles written about you
- Newspaper/Magazine/Journal articles written by you
- A brochure describing the speaker and their programs, products or services
- A sample of the speaker's product (CD, DVD or book)
- Past event evaluations
- Past customer evaluation comments about the speaker
- Proposal outlining a sample presentation
- Glossy professional photograph of the speaker

The Speaker's One-Sheet

This is the best promotional item in the MPK. Usually printed on 8.5" x 11" white glossy paper stock, the one-sheet is a color advertisement for you and your work. It usually features your picture in a professional pose, or it could be a regular headshot. The page may also include other images of you on stage, or images of your products. The copy on the one-sheet is promotional in nature, and designed to persuade a potential client to hire you.

Many speakers just starting out will print this document out on their own color laser printer to save money. If you choose to do this, be sure to have it reviewed by several professionals to be sure that your one-sheet looks professional rather than cheap and/or homemade. To see different formats for this MPK item, do an internet search using the words *speaker* and *one-sheet*.

The CV

The initials CV stand for *Curriculum Vitae*. It's a specific type of resume usually found in the academic and medical/research arenas. It differs from a resume which is a condensed, chronological list of a person's employment history coupled with a brief synopsis of skills. A resume is often made to fit on no more than two pages. A Curriculum Vitae, on the other hand, provides an overview of a person's experience, qualifications, publications, accomplishments, awards, etc., and can be as many pages long as are needed to list all the pertinent information.

One of the reasons a CV works so well for entrepreneurs, consultants, speakers, and sales professionals is because they can accommodate diverse and unique backgrounds. Some people start their businesses at a very early age – and their CV's would reflect that, but it's when a person discovers their passion and their message that they are more likely to start thinking about speaking and sharing with others. The flexible format of the CV allows you to include items that might be pertinent to your expertise, but are not directly related to speaking.

If you need some help or guidance with drafting your own CV, or want to see samples of actual CVs, there's a lot of information available both on the internet and in books.

Letters of Recommendation

Also known as referral letters, or letters of reference, these important documents are testimonies from clients and customers relating their personal experience with what you do and how well you do it. These letters are excellent additions to your MPK because they show potential clients what previous clients thought about you and your work.

We've already talked about these letters, so I'll just provide you with a few reminders:

- Even if you're just starting out and still speaking for free, ask your contacts if they would be willing to write you a referral letter.
- Make sure any speaker's agreement (chapter 16) you use includes a request for a letter of reference written on the organization's or company's letterhead.
- Call your contact person one week after the event and politely remind them that you were hoping for a letter of reference.
- If your contact is having trouble writing the letter, offer to send them a sample letter.
- If your contact doesn't feel comfortable writing the letter because they weren't in the audience, suggest that they talk to someone who was in the audience and ask them for their comments.

Above all, be kind, be patient, and only send one reminder. Cherish the letters you get and let go of thoughts about the ones you weren't able to get.

Newspaper, Journal or Magazine Articles Written About You

There's an old adage that says: "There's no such thing as bad press." As untrue as this general statement is about getting your name in print, there's still an element of truth to it. As a speaker, you will certainly get your name in print as the result of your talks, and you'll want to add those clippings to your MPK. But, like most people, you'll also get your name in print for other things worth capturing.

For example, if your expertise is in the medical field and there was an article and a picture published in a journal about your receiving an award from a medical organization, you could include that article in your MPK. If your expertise is in the field of children's activities, and a local newspaper runs a story about you volunteering your time as a reader at an elementary school, this too would be an excellent addition to your MPK.

Being acknowledged and covered by print media for situations, activities, awards, or accomplishments related to your field of expertise shows that your professionalism and interest in your topic extends beyond the stage. It's something you share with the community too. It also means that someone heard about you, or about something you were going to be doing or participating in, and decided it was newsworthy. Even if their coverage was influenced by a press release you sent out, it's still the result of someone's decision. That's why articles written about you make such a good impression on potential clients. It's not you tooting your own horn; it's someone else.

When you do get coverage and your story ends up in print, buy copies of the newspaper, journal or magazine, clip the articles, and ad them to your MPK.

Newspaper, Journal or Magazine Articles Written By You

Whether you are a new speaker or a seasoned veteran, any article you're able to get into print is an article you can consider adding to your MPK. As your speaking career progresses though, you will have more published articles to choose from. Choose articles that are closely related to your speaking topics. If you speak about business etiquette, the article you wrote about your amazing garden might not be appropriate even if it did end up being printed in a prestigious publication.

Again, when your work ends up in print, buy copies of the newspaper, journal or magazine, clip the articles, and ad them to your kit.

A Professionally Designed Brochure on You and Your Programs

Some speakers decide to include a brochure in their MPK. In general, it has a lot of the same information as the one-sheet, but because it's a two-sided document there's also a lot more room to provide an expanded list of your programs, products, and services. For example, I provide a brochure about the specialized training I offer to parents and parent educators.

If you have additional products and services that you'd like to accentuate, then a professionally designed, color, tri-fold brochure may be just what you need. An additional advantage to having a brochure is that it's also an excellent marketing tool that you can hand out when you are speaking.

The one word of advice here is to use a professional printing service. There are do-it-yourself brochure kits available at your local office supply store, but unless you have experience with creating brochures, they're more likely to end up looking like they're homemade rather than professional.

Sample Product

Speakers who passionately and confidently step on a stage can influence, motivate, and inspire their audiences to take action in their own lives. One way to help your audience members keep the momentum moving in a positive direction after your presentation is to provide them with a variety of products they can purchase to take home with them. We will be covering the creation of products like books, CDs, and DVDs in later chapters. There is also a later chapter that explains what "back-of-the-room sales" are and how you can use them to extend your professional reach.

Once you have a product or two, they can be added to your MPK. I often include a copy of my book when the MPK is being hand delivered. On my website, I can't provide a copy of my book, but I do include a variety of current video clips that show me in action.

Past Event Performance Evaluations

Becoming a better speaker happens as the result of being able to evaluate past performances in terms of what worked, what didn't work, and what you can do to improve or fix your presentations. One of the best tools for collecting information about our speaking skills is a written evaluation form filled out by members of your audience. It isn't always appropriate or convenient to ask your audience for evaluations, like when you are speaking at a luncheon or a club meeting, but there will be plenty of opportunities to get audience feedback.

The best approach is to ask your contact if they have some type of evaluation form that they use to get feedback from their participants. If they don't have one, ask them if they would mind if you handed out an evaluation form that you use. If they say no, that's okay; let it go. If they say yes to your form, you can offer to share the information collected from the evaluations with them after the event.

A lot of events already have an evaluation form they like to use. For them, it's a tool that helps determine whether or not a speaker might be invited back. If they do have their own evaluation system in place, ask your contact if you will be able to review the information collected. Sometimes they will send you the evaluation results as a brief multi-page handout. If it reflects an overall positive performance, consider duplicating it and including it in your MPK. I added an evaluation summary I received to both my off and online MPKs. The numbers in it are very good, but the comments are great. If you'd like to have a look at it, it's part of my online MPK and it's titled: *Conference Keynote Evaluation*.

Past Customer Comments

Whether you're shopping for a book on Amazon.com or searching for a restaurant on Yelp.com, if you're like me, you read the customer comments. There are always a small percentage of bad reviews, but they might have been the result of a really bad day for the individual rather than being a true reflection of the product or service. What I look for is all those other comments; are they good – positive - positively glowing?

Positive customer comments can be just as powerful as letters of recommendation and evaluation summaries. When select comments are compiled into a single sheet and included in your MPK, they are additional evidence that you are an engaging and interesting speaker. I have a single sheet of customer comments in my offline MPK titled: "Read What People are Saying about Bill Corbett's Presentations." You can also post positive customer comments on your website.

Your Sample Presentation Proposal

Placing a sample of a proposal in your MPK gives a prospective client a detailed view of one of your products or services. It includes a brief synopsis, a detailed outline of what you will be presenting, and biographical information about you.

If you've ever heard of the idea that you should 'act-as-if,' this is one of those times when acting-as-if can get you hired. When you're just starting out, you may not have an actual client to create a proposal for, but that's no reason to wait. Start writing your proposals now. At the very least, you will have all the preliminary work done so that when someone does ask you for a formal proposal, you won't be stressed out by the thought of having to create one from scratch. Once you've finished your first sample, you can add it to both MPKs. It may turn out to be exactly what someone was looking for.

Professional Headshot or Photograph

Human beings are curious creatures and when it comes to working with people, we want to know what they look like. As a rule though, the idea of sitting for a professional 'headshot' is not a pleasant thought for a lot of people. Super models aside, most people think they take terrible pictures. But successful speakers aren't hired because of their looks; they're hired because they are knowledgeable, informative, and can engage their audience from their first to their last word. The truth is, passion is beautiful.

When prospective clients are considering hiring you, they will make a few preliminary observations about you from your photo that have nothing to do with how handsome or beautiful you are. They will decide if you are well groomed and look clean. They will look at the clothes you chose to wear. They will look at the quality of the photo. The way you present yourself in a photo isn't a true representation of the whole person that you are, but it is a reflection of how much of a professional you consider yourself to be.

The headshot is a professional photo of a person from the chest up. Sometimes your headshot is going to be the first image of you that someone sees. So unless you are a professional photographer, this is one of those times when it pays to go to someone who is a professional photographer. Using a homemade picture captured with a cell phone puts you at risk for being considered as amateurish and unprofessional as the picture might be.

Having a headshot done does not have to be expensive. Do some networking to find photographers in your area. Check out their websites and call around to find one that will shoot your headshot for a reasonable price. You might even find a photographer who is also just starting out and willing to take your headshot at a very reasonable price. I have gotten professional headshots done for around $50. Bartering may be another alternative way of getting your headshot. Do you have any products or services you might be able to offer in exchange for the photo?

When you have your picture, make sure to get a black and white 5" x 7" copy to include in your MPK. With the capabilities and quality of today's home computers and printers, you should be able to scan your photo into your computer and duplicate it to create copies for your physical MPKs. You can also upload your photo from your computer into your online MPK. And, although this is not a requirement, consider putting your headshot with your bio, your CV, and/or your sample proposal.

Putting It All Together

Now that you know about the various items that can be used to fill out your MPK, you'll need something to physically hold them together - the folder. I like to use glossy, two-pocket report folders that can be found at just about any office supply store. The glossy folder gives your MPK a clean professional look. A good time to buy them is July thru September when school supplies go on sale.

If you feel comfortable with straight lines, you can use your computer to create folder labels that provide all of your contact information. The one thing you'll want to make sure of though, is that the label is accurately positioned on the front cover. A crooked label won't do. If you don't like the idea of struggling to affix labels to your folders, you can order folders with all of your information preprinted on the cover from online print companies like VistaPrint.com.

In the beginning, your MPK might be thin, but now you have a lot of strategies for filling it up. Start with what you have and add as you go along. Every time you have an item you are thinking about including, review what you already have and remove items that are out-of date or no longer applicable.

My first marketing/press kit consisted of a one-sheet, my CV, and a sample presentation proposal. Remember, potential clients won't always be impressed by the thickness of your MPK; they will be impressed by the quality and professionalism of the way you present yourself.

Now that you've done a lot of the off-the-stage work, it's time to talk about on-stage opportunities and how to make the most of them. But first, here's a list of action items:

Action Items:

- Go to www.BillCorbett.com and click on the Press/Media tab to see my MPK items
- Use the internet to find examples of other speaker's one-sheet
- Begin drafting your own one-sheet and seek out feedback from people whose business opinion you respect
- Seek out internet resources and books for examples of CVs
- Ask other professionals to share their CVs with you
- Begin drafting your own CV and seek out feedback from people whose business opinion you respect
- Collect articles written about you or by you, and make photocopies for your MPK
- Begin drafting a proposal for a presentation you are ready to give
- Find a photographer and make an appointment to get your headshot
- Purchase glossy, two-pocket report folders to have on hand so you can assemble your MPKs
- Create folder labels with your name (or your business name) and all of your contact information, or order

your preprinted folders so that you will have them on hand when you need them

Chapter 15

When the Calls Start Coming In

Being Ready to Talk About What You Have to Offer

Now that people have both a reason and a way to get in touch with you, they are also going to want more details about you and what you have to offer. The interesting reality is that you're going to want more details about them too.

One thing you can do to prepare for initial contacts is to create a Contact Information Sheet you can fill out while you're speaking with them. This sheet should include prompts and spaces to write down information about your contact, the event, and any other details you feel are important. This way you'll always have your notes to refer to rather than having to make an unnecessary, potentially embarrassing phone call just because you can't remember something.

These notes are also a way to refresh your memory before speaking with a client you haven't spoken to recently. Sometimes, the details you were able to capture during your initial conversation will really impress people when they hear them several months later. At the very least, they're proof you know how to listen.

The Proposal

In chapter 5 we covered creating your content as a process of listing everything you know in your general topic area, grouping those ideas into specific topics you would enjoy speaking about, and then building outlines which can be used as templates for your talks. The great thing about these outlines is that now you can also use them as part of your proposals.

A proposal is a detailed plan of the products and/or services you are offering to potential clients. It includes all the Who, What, Where, When, How, and Why of how you can help them. At this point, you already have a lot of the information you will need to generate a proposal. The actual 'how to put it together' instructions can be found with an internet search, or in books you can find in your local libraries (although this may be one of those times when it's easier to have an actual book in your hand to follow).

The goal of your proposal is to give your potential clients a reason to take action and hire you. You've already made a good impression whether it's the result of a referral, a face to face meeting, or from someone sitting in one of your audiences; but now you need to let them know what you have to offer so they can decide if you're a good match for their clients and customers. Your proposal will help them make that decision.

One thing to remember though, sometimes your initial proposal will just be a starting point for the hiring conversation. Be prepared to adjust your proposal to address your client's questions, concerns, issues, and/or logistics.

You can also use some of the information you are generating for the proposal, on your website. Consider adding a tab on your webpage that will list your primary topics along with a brief outline for each topic. Be sure to include enough detailed information so that when people find your list, they know what you are currently prepared to speak about.

You can also use this webpage to send potential clients to; but don't swap a chance to talk about what you have to offer with sending them to your website. Letting them know you have an online topic list is just another way to get them to your website so they can learn more about you. And, don't be concerned with how many topics you have listed. Too many topics might make you appear too generic. A few specific, well thought out topics might just make a better impression.

What to Charge Your Clients

One question you are going to need to prepare an answer for is: "What is your fee?" Almost every event has a budget. This means that meeting planners and event coordinators will need to know how much you are going to charge them so they can decide if you fit within their budget constraints. They probably won't expect you to tell them how much your appearance will cost during the initial contact. They will understand that you need more details about the event first. But any proposal you submit will certainly need to include the fee; and sooner or later, you're going to have to come up with a basic fee structure that you're comfortable with.

When I was just starting my speaking career, determining what to charge was a huge hurdle to get over. In the very beginning I spoke for free to build confidence in my ability, but it was also because it was hard to believe that people would be willing to pay actual money to hear me speak.

Making the decision to start charging a fee isn't something that happens after a specific amount of time or after a specific number of events; it's different for everybody. One guideline you might use to help you decide when it's time to start charging a speaking fee is the response of your audience. When that first person comes up to you and tells you how meaningful your message was to them, and you see that spark in them, that's when it's time to start thinking about setting up a fee structure.

When I was ready to make the shift from 'free-to-fee,' I set a starting rate of $50 per half hour. That rate immediately resulted in my getting $150 for a 90 minute presentation which seemed very fair at the time. One thing you DON'T want to do is publish your rate anywhere except in the proposal or on the invoices you give directly to your client. This is the best way to avoid the complications of one group accidentally finding out how much less a similar group was charged.

When you do decide on a fee structure, whether it's hourly, by the day, or situation specific, try to be consistent. Set your initial fees so that you feel they are equal in value to your confidence and skill level. As you improve, raise them. People do get paid excellent money to share their knowledge and expertise. When you become a qualified and confident speaker with a great message, you become one of those people and you deserve to be adequately compensated.

If there's ever a time when you decide you'd like to lower your rates to accommodate a new client, a new topic, or a new program, you can always offer a 'limited time special price.' The rule of thumb is that it's always easier to adjust your fees lower by offering a discount than it is to try and raise your fee after you disclosed it.

Action Items:

- Seek out resources on how to write a proposal
- Add a page to your website that provides detailed information about your talks
- Decide what your starting fee will be so you'll be ready when clients ask

Chapter 16

Getting Commitment with a Speaker's Agreement

When you do secure your first paid speaking gig, you'll want a way to keep track of all the details. Some details are basic, like knowing where to go, what time to be there, where to park, and who will pay you once you're done. Other details provide important information about your audience, the specifics of what you will be presenting to them, and the time logistics of the format.

In my earliest years as a speaker, I remember being so overwhelmed with the excitement of getting hired that I actually forgot some of the event details. I'd go back to the notes I'd taken during the initial interview only to realize that they didn't have anywhere near as much information as I thought they did.

I remember one event I was hired to speak at that was taking place in a large hall in a downtown area. I worked very hard on my presentation and my delivery, and was convinced I was going to 'knock their socks off' with my talk. On the day of the event I received a phone call from my event contact reminding me that the event had been moved to another location. I discreetly mentioned that I had not been aware of the change and was very thankful that had she called me to let me know. She said she was sure she had sent me a message informing me of the change. After our conversation, I checked and double checked emails and phone messages, but couldn't find any evidence that I had received that information.

I could have shown her my proof that I hadn't been informed of the change in location, but in the end, it's my job to show up in the right place at the right time. Fortunately for both of us, the event took place without issue. But this incident was a wake-up call for me as a professional to do everything within my power to prevent the likelihood of miscommunication between myself and my client regarding the details of an event.

As a direct result of that experience, I decided to use a Speaker's Agreement with all future speaking gigs. Used by many top-notch professional speakers, this agreement is drawn up between you and your customer as a way of recording all the agreed upon details of the event. By using it, you reduce the chances of missing or losing vital information, you are able to make sure that your expectations are in alignment with your client's expectations, and you minimize the likelihood of any future misunderstandings between you and your client.

Because it is an agreement initiated by you, it may not be considered a legally binding document. Still, it definitely reveals you as a professional while encouraging your client to be similarly professional by honoring their commitments as per the agreement that you both signed.

The agreement I use has evolved and improved over the years. The original version was generously provided by motivational speaker, friend, and mentor Bill Karlson – www.BillKarlson.com – and is still reflected in the core of my version. Over the years though, my agreement has changed to include elements specific to my audience, and as the result of sharing information and format ideas with other speakers. I have included it in the Appendix located in the back of this book so you can see how well it captures all the details of an event. Feel free to use it as the basis of your own speaker's agreement.

When I send it to potential clients, I make sure all of my current contact information is filled in at the top of the agreement. From that point forward, the client fills in the blanks. The result is a document with all the details of the event as provided by the client.

Once you receive the completed agreement from your contact, go over it to make sure all the information provided matches up with your own notes. If it does, sign it and send a copy back to the contact. Make another copy and then store the original document someplace safe.

Use the copy as your reference while you are preparing for the event and make sure to bring it with you on the day of the event. It contains all the event contact information you might need, including an emergency phone number. This is the number you would call on the day of the event if you were lost, were arriving later than expected, or were having trouble getting into the building. I've had to use that emergency number a few times for locked buildings, locked rooms, or because someone forgot to notify the person in charge of the facility that an event had been scheduled.

It may seem strange to require so much information, but there's nothing worse than arriving at an event and realizing you don't have something you planned on having. For example, I require the availability of a lavaliere microphone, the type you wear on your lapel, because I use props throughout my presentations and need my hands free. You'll see that I have the microphone requirement listed in my speaker's agreement.

Toward the end of the agreement I also provide a checklist for the client. They check each item to confirm that they can – or cannot – provide each item on the list. It's an excellent way to eliminate any misunderstandings. If it turns out that they cannot provide something I need, then I know that I'll have to make other arrangements.

Each part of the speaker's agreement plays a role in setting the stage for a successful talk. When you're just getting started, plan for the highest level of success by capturing as many details about the event as you can in the agreement. This doesn't mean using it as a way to get the event to do all the work. It's just an excellent way of divvying up the responsibilities so everyone knows what's expected of them. Without a speaker's agreement, you and your client will be at the mercy of assumptions about who's going to do what, and we all know how that usually plays out.

Section

III

Chapter 17

The Conference

They are called by a variety of names: conferences, conventions, exhibitions, expos, annual meetings, company retreats, events, etc., but they all basically have the same premise. They are designed to bring together a group of people to share, experience, listen, and learn. Throughout this book I've been referring to these gatherings as conferences, but only because that's what the events I usually speak at are called. An event specific to your topic might be called an expo. Just to be consistent, I'm going to continue to refer to them as conferences.

Most conferences are annual events. There are a few that are held semi-annually, but they're likely to be providing mandatory training hours and are held twice a year to accommodate work schedules and/or licensing requirements. Regardless of whether a conference is held once or twice a year, the main goal of the planning committee is to ensure that the content will meet the needs of the people attending. To achieve this goal, they will do their best to design an event that speakers, trainers, vendors, and anyone else interested in the topic will find interesting, engaging, productive, and worth the cost of admission.

As your knowledge of your topic grows, you will begin to hear about the different conferences your potential clients attend. Go online and find conference websites. Look at their agendas, program guides, and list of breakout/workshop speakers. Go to the speaker's websites too. Sometimes speakers have their upcoming engagements listed on their website calendar. When they do, you may discover events you haven't heard of yet.

Most conferences try to provide a variety of speakers in an effort to get good coverage of the topic. Part of this process is dividing potential speakers into tiers. Large conferences may have three tiers: the entry level breakout/workshop speakers, a small select group of featured speakers, and then the featured keynote speaker. Very small conferences may have no more than a handful of speakers. There are no rules about how many speakers an event should have. Organizers make their decisions based on the budgets they've been given and how much topic coverage they're trying to achieve.

When you're getting started, being one of the breakout/workshop speakers at a conference is a great opportunity to get exposure. It's also very rewarding because your audience will be filled with people who chose your workshop from a list of workshops all being offered at the same time. If they chose to sit in on your workshop, it's because they want to hear what you have to say.

In the next two chapters we will be covering techniques you can incorporate into your presentation to engage your workshop audiences and keep them captivated throughout. Taking the time to learn these techniques and then implementing them will help your audiences connect with both you and your information. They will also help you become more skilled at mastering the stage of any event.

Chapter 18

Winning Over Your Audience

Have you ever attended an event where the speaker clearly knew their material but failed at keeping their audience interested and engaged in what they were saying? Instead, people talked, yawned, checked their watches, snuck out, or turned to electronic devices. That type of presentation is like a one-way conversation with the speaker doing all the talking and the audience too bored to listen.

Engaging the audience is one of a speaker's main goals. In their book, *The Big Book of Presentation Games*, authors Scannell & Newstrom write about the importance of capturing an audience's attention with activities that engage them as opposed to just lecturing to them. They refer to studies that talk about how short people's attention spans can be and how it's up to us to build presentations filled with "life and variety."

They're right. Human beings never do well sitting still for long periods of time, especially when all they're required to do is listen to one person's voice. They may share the same basic interest in what you have to say, but as individuals, they bring their own unspoken expectations and individual learning styles into the room with them.

As a speaker with a message to share, it's up to you to figure out how to engage them in ways that will help them absorb the material you are presenting. Fortunately, there is a lot of information on different ways of doing that.

Sharing – Making Allies, not Enemies, in Your Workshop

People enjoy helping out. If you have information or worksheets to hand out, call on people who arrive early to help pass them out. If part of your presentation involves asking your audience to contribute to lists of things, ask for a volunteer to write the information on the board or flip chart at the front of the room. Occasionally I'll ask parents and teachers in my workshop to share the challenges they are having with their children. I have a volunteer write them on the board so that I can move about the room and establish a better connection with my audience.

Create opportunities. The people coming into your workshop have years of personal experience and some would love to share it. One thing you can do is to ask your audience questions and then respond to their answers in a way that makes them feel like they made a valuable contribution. If you get an unexpected answer that doesn't quite fit the question or presents a point of view that you don't support, find at least one positive aspect of the answer and acknowledge it.

People like talking to each other. Design your presentation with at least one break-out exercise that has the audience working with a neighbor or together in small groups. For example: give them a topic related issue they've all had to deal with and have them come up with as many creative solutions as they can. Then, allow them to share their ideas with the rest of the group.

Respect for Your Audience

People aren't going to walk into your presentation wondering how much respect you have for them, but in a way, they are your guests. You have invited them in to listen to information you believe they will benefit from. By remembering to extend a few simple courtesies, you will be letting them know that you appreciate their choosing to attend your presentation, and that you value their time as much as you value your own.

- Be in your workshop room when your participants arrive. If you are able, greet them as they enter.
- Wear a name tag to let them know who you are or reveal your identity on the board or flip chart located at the front of the room.
- When you're working with volunteers, use their names. If they aren't wearing name tags, ask them for their name before you begin working with them.
- Start your workshop on time even though people will be walking in late. This shows respect for those who did arrive on time, and they will appreciate not being made to wait.
- Be sure to follow your handouts and bring attention to any changes you've made to them before you get started. If you don't, members of your audience will become distracted while trying to figure out if they're on the right page – or not.
- Announce 'housekeeping' details before you begin: the start and stop times, times for scheduled breaks (if there are any), rules for cell phones, location of restrooms, etc.
- If there are breaks planned, try to arrange your presentation so that scheduled breaks occur at a natural stopping point between two pieces of information.
- Plan your talk to end at the designated time. People don't like it when the speaker runs out of time and isn't able to make it through all the information they were supposed to cover. Going over your allotted time is not only disrespectful to your audience and their schedule; it's also disrespectful to the presenters following you.

Role Playing

Role play exercises can be an effective way to get your point across. Discreetly find volunteers for any role playing exercises you have planned before your workshop begins. If you want them to do something specific, make sure to provide them with clear and specific instructions.

In my early years of presenting, I decided to construct a role play with two adults pretending to be my children. I wanted them to act out a specific situation involving sibling rivalry so that I could approach them and show my participants how to defuse the situation. One of the most important requirements for this exercise to work was to have my 'children' sitting next to each other in the chairs I had set up on stage so I could perform my 'magic' in close proximity to them.

When the exercise started, it all went terribly wrong! Both adults got up from their chairs and began to run around the room chasing each other. They played their roles as children too well and the demonstration I had planned was ruined because I had failed to give them clear and concise instructions; I left out the part where they were supposed to remain seated in their chairs. My audience wasn't aware of my mistake though, and broke out into laughter which in turn fueled my volunteer's disruptive behavior. For the next few minutes, I had very little control over the room. My volunteers did eventually return to their chairs and I was able to regain control. But I had lost the opportunity to get my point across and had to deal with the fact that it was due to my mistake.

Finding your volunteers beforehand provides you with enough time to go over what you'd like them to do. It also avoids putting people on the spot or unknowingly calling on someone who dislikes being called on. When the role play is over, always make sure to audibly thank your volunteers and initiate applause from the audience in recognition of their willingness to participate.

Learning Styles

Lecturing is one of the methods you will be using to deliver material to your audience. It might even be the preferred way for a few, but not everyone enjoys learning the same way. Research shows that the learning preferences people develop are a blend of the ways they were taught at home, in school, in the community, and of their own natural preferences for how they best absorb what they are learning. Good workshop presenters acknowledge that people learn differently and incorporate a variety of techniques to make their content more accessible and memorable to their audience.

The Visual Learner

These are people who enjoy learning by watching or looking at the information being provided. If there are words being spoken while they are viewing, they will be absorbed as part of the learning process too, but most of the information will be absorbed visually. A few examples of techniques for reaching visual learners include: graphics in your PowerPoint, videos, the use of props, and instances of role play.

Sometimes it's so easy to plan for the visual learner that your presentation could end up with too many graphics or videos. An excess of graphics might make your content look skimpy and unprofessional. Too many videos might take time away from interacting with your audience. Videos can also be problematic when it comes to time constraints and computer performance.

Props can be fun to use and can enhance your audience's ability to connect with the material being presented by evoking memories, experiences, or emotions. After adding a real wooden paddle to my presentation on alternatives to spanking, many participates told me about how all the emotions of being spanked as a child came back to them as soon as they saw that paddle in my hand. Props can be powerful, but they can also cause distractions or contribute to you losing credibility if they aren't used carefully.

Years ago I began using a toolbox as a metaphor for the toolbox of discipline tools parents' use. After arriving at an out-of-town conference, I realized I'd left my toolbox prop at home and quickly ran to a local hardware store to purchase one. The weight and shape of this new box was different from the one I was used to. As a result, when I took the heaviest tool out of the box, it became unbalanced and fell off the table and onto the floor with a resounding crash. Not only did it startle me, but my audience began to laugh. I learned the hard way to handle my props more carefully, especially ones that were new to me.

When you choose to work with props, always practice with them until you have absolute confidence with the ways you will be using them. Even when you're confident, continue to practice regularly.

Auditory Learners

When people think of auditory learners, they tend to immediately think of teachers and professors standing in front of a class and lecturing, but there are other types of auditory experiences people enjoy, one of them being music. As a speaker, you have the option of using music to create an atmosphere in your room even before your workshop presentation starts.

Music can be activated by playing a CD in a portable CD player or in the CD drive of a laptop. You can embed music files into your PowerPoint presentations and program them to start and stop according to your own design. With an Apple iPhone you can utilize Bluetooth technology to send a signal to an iPhone compatible wireless speaker. Then, with the iPhone in hand, you can start and stop the music, increase or decrease the volume, change songs, etc.

I once conducted a workshop on presentation skills at a large company. I had purchased a piece of music that represented the mood I wanted to create for my one hour lecture – an enticing mystery. The piece was instrumental and consisted of soft drums and flutes. I embedded the music in my PowerPoint presentation and started playing it about 20 minutes before the workshop began.

As I greeted people entering the room, the music played softly on the surround sound speakers in the lecture hall. The music helped set the mood I intentionally wanted to create. When the workshop had ended, one man approached me and asked me for the title of the music. He described how intrigued he'd felt listening to it while waiting in line to enter. My mission had been accomplished; I had set the mood and engaged at least one more participant before they even entered the room.

As a child behavior specialist, many of my audiences are comprised of parents and teachers. The mood I like to set for those workshops is fun and child-like so the music I like to use is of children singing or folk songs about childhood activities.

In the middle of one of my workshops, I ask everyone to take a quick test. They have two minutes to complete it and half way through the exercise, I hit the remote button on my laptop and the theme from the popular television game show Jeopardy starts playing. My audience always breaks into laughter.

Audiences Appreciate Your Efforts

However you decide to implement this information into your presentation, each has its own capacity to hold your audience's attention while you continue to share your valuable content. They've already told you they are interested in hearing what you have to say by walking into the room. Now you have some ideas of how to better meet their expectations. You'll get a feel for how well you did by the number of people waiting around after your presentation to share their thoughts and to get more information about you and your products and services.

Chapter 19

Teaching Methods for
Connecting with Your Audience

The last chapter focused on your presentation from the audience's perspective and offered some insight into their expectations as well as information on how to accommodate a few learning style preferences. This chapter focuses on the presentation from *your* perspective as a teacher with a desire to share your information in ways that your audience will respond to.

Case Studies: Case studies are in-depth examinations of a person, group, or situation, and are used to report research in the social and life science fields. The advantage of using case studies is that they often do a very good job of using real life examples to explain complex theories. When you include information gathered from case studies and research in your presentation, it helps build a foundation that supports your message and increases your credibility with your audience.

If case studies are available and applicable to your topic area, you'll want to stay current with what's being published. If you don't, you run the risk of your audience knowing more than you do.

Storytelling and Anecdotes: The difference between talking about case studies and sharing stories and personal anecdotes is that stories and anecdotes tend to be more social and casual. They are the kinds of things we might hear about over drinks or dinner or around the water cooler at work. For a speaker, they help close the distance between the stage and the audience, especially when they are about you.

Remember in Chapter 6 when I told you about the first time I spoke and how my knees were shaking so much that I was afraid I was going to fall down in front my audience of 150 people? When I tell audiences that story now, they laugh. And that's good because I don't want them to feel bad for me; I want them to know that everything turned out okay. I don't have to worry about my knees anymore, and I'm speaking to them now so they can learn techniques for overcoming the dreaded 'Shaky Knee Syndrome.'

The stories and anecdotes you pick can bring your content to life. Like any other technique though, use them sparingly and with the permission of anyone else featured in them.

Breakout Exercises: Another popular teaching method is to break your audience into smaller groups and assign each group a topic related problem to solve. Make sure they know how much time they have to work together and provide them with time prompts so they can finish their work on time. While they're working on their problems, you can visit each group to see if they have any questions or need any clarification. When the time allotted for the exercise is up, have each group select a spokesperson to report their group's results to the rest of the audience.

Handouts: There are a few good reasons to use handouts:

- They can be set up in the form of an outline to provide participants with a way to keep their notes organized over the course of the workshop.
- They help your audience stay in sync with your presentation.
- When your participants leave, they will have their structured notes to refer to later on.

- You can take advantage of the header and footer areas of the handout as a place to provide your contact information.
- People learn better when they take notes. When all they do is listen, the information they've heard has a tendency to go in one ear and out the other.

It's true that it costs money to print handouts, but it's well worth the effort and the expense. To make the most of them:

- Organize your handouts so they accurately follow your presentation.
- Keep the information you provide in bullet-like sentences. If you provide too much information, participants won't have a reason to take notes.
- Make sure you provide enough room below the bullets for participants to write on.

Your handouts can be any number of pages; it's your choice. To figure out how much written information to provide versus how much information you want them to record, take the time to write down everything you want your audience to walk away with. Go back through what you've written to pull out your outline headings and any specific pieces of information you want to include. You'll also be able to see how much writing room you need to provide.

If you are using PowerPoint or charts, make sure the information compliments the information in the handouts. By the end of your presentation, your participants should have a handout filled with your valuable information to take home.

Questions: A good way to keep a workshop interesting is to check in with your audience by asking open ended questions (a question that requires more than a yes or no answer). Your questions will also give you a feel for whether or not the audience is 'getting it.' Sometimes one person will speak up and say something and half the audience will be nodding their heads in agreement. Thanks to their peer, they now have another opportunity to develop a clearer understanding of the material being presented.

Questions can also be used as a way to focus your audience's attention. I often ask my audiences questions after they return from breaks as a way to remind them of the last thing we discussed.

Guests and Panels of Experts: Invite other experts onto your stage to share their information, experience, and perspective. Your audience will appreciate the chance to hear from other experts, and respect you for caring enough about your topic to make sure that they get a lot of quality information. You get the opportunity and the privilege of working with other experts.

As a child behavior expert, I often get opportunities to share the stage. One of the greatest benefits of these situations is the level of professionalism people perceive when they see experts with similar interests working together. Sometimes it's easy to call yourself an expert, but hard to convince others that it's true. Sharing a stage, or being on or in charge of a panel of experts, can help solidify your professional status. It also adds value and gives your audience another reason to be engaged throughout the presentation.

I once presented at a state wide conference on early childhood education. My workshop was about discipline tools that can be used in both the home and the classroom. The audience was all teachers, and I knew they would wonder about my ability to relate to their issues when my real life experience was as a parent.

As a proactive measure, I decided to address their questions and concerns before they even had a chance to voice them by inviting three seasoned early childhood teachers to appear as a panel of experts. They each new my work and were able to validate my assumptions with their input and answers. The session was a huge success!

There is one challenge when it comes to working with your fellow experts/professionals – confidence. When you're just starting out, it may be intimidating to think about asking a colleague to work with you, but don't let a lack of stage experience interfere with the confidence you have when it comes to your topic.

Working with others also helps you avoid being thought of as a know-it-all or falling into the trap of thinking you know it all. A willingness to hear what your colleagues have to offer shows that you are confident about the quality of the material you bring to the table. We are always learning and growing. Having good relationships with our fellow professionals just enhances that process.

Surprises: In his book *No Sweat Public Speaking*, speaker, author, and presentation skills coach, Fred Miller, encourages speakers to do something unusual to get their audience's attention and help them remember the point being made.

> Delivering something unexpected usually catches the attention quicker, and is remembered longer than the same-old, same-old. Something unusual might be the handling of a prop, a unique series of gestures, or even wearing a costume or uniform to emphasize something... (Miller, 2011)

This teaching method can be incredibly effective when handled professionally, carefully, and with a lot of planning and practice. It should also be something directly related to your topic. The object is to surprise your audience with someone or something that unexpectedly occurs in the workshop. The benefit of using the element of surprise is that it can be an experiential and memorable way for your audience to learn something.

A while back, I was hired to conduct a three hour lecture for 50 fathers and their sons about how fathers can guide and help their sons to get in touch with their feelings. I knew it was going to be a challenging audience because we were going to be covering parenting concepts, the idea of emotional intelligence, and generally going into areas men don't usually go into by choice. I decided to use the element of surprise and invited my 25 year old son to join me on stage for that event.

The plan was for my son to hide in the audience. I was introduced by the event organizer as the session's only presenter and I began my talk. At just the right moment, my tall lanky son with his baggy jeans and baseball cap cocked to the side, left his seat in the audience, walked up the steps and onto the stage where he proceeded to interrupt my presentation. His opening challenge was "Hold on, do you really expect these guys to believe what you're saying? Feelings... they have to allow their sons to feel their feelings?"

The staged interruption went off without a hitch, and it soon turned into a somewhat heated verbal debate on stage. The men in the audience were stunned that someone was challenging the presenter, even though the young man was apparently taking their side and questioning the different kinds of parenting techniques being explained. We stopped our debate after a few minutes and both turned to the audience so I could introduce my son to the group. Applause broke out and we went on to share the stage as co-presenters for the remainder of the event.

If you do decide to use the element of surprise, plan it carefully because if you don't, it can be an epic fail. If you plan to use another person, think of it as a very short play and commit to learning your lines and stage positions by heart. If you plan to use an object or some type of special effect, practice, practice, practice, and then practice some more.

A Memorable Workshop

Over the past two chapters, I've given you a lot of information and ideas about different ways to enhance the likelihood of your audiences enjoying and benefiting from your workshops and presentations. It'll take you a little time to decide which techniques are best suited for your style and material. It's also likely that you will come up with your own adaptations and ideas from watching other speakers. It is a learning process.

Try different techniques, make sure the content you are using is yours, and become an expert with the ones you are most comfortable with. You'll be rewarded when you see members of your audience experience those wonderful 'ah-ha' moments that just don't seem to happen with a boring lecture. And remember, each new thing you learn about and utilize to make your presentations stand out, moves you one step closer to the keynote stage.

Chapter 20

The Keynote

Before deciding to build your own speaking business, you may have thought like a lot of people do, that to be a keynote speaker you need to be some type of celebrity. There are celebrities who become speakers as a result of their expert status in the topic covered, and there are celebrities who come from a different area with a specific interest in the topic covered. But you don't need to be a celebrity to be a keynote speaker; you do need to be an expert in your field.

There is a conference I attend regularly that has had both celebrity and non-celebrity keynotes. Recently, I heard a local school principal deliver an excellent keynote speech. When he finished, he received a very enthusiastic standing ovation.

Many organizations that put on conferences don't have the budget to bring in high-priced celebrities or renowned experts, at least not every year. This is when speakers like you and I can get our chance to showcase our talent and knowledge. Still, it's up to us to get the ball rolling by providing the speaker search committee with two types of information they will want before considering us: personal recommendations from known or respected sources and our professional marketing/press kit (covered in chapter 14).

How to Get on the Speaker Search Committee's Radar

The more often you speak in front of audiences - large, small, free, or paid - the more you increase your chances of getting noticed, talked about, and recommended. Therefore, the number one method for building your excellent reputation is to speak, speak, speak, and then speak some more! Always strive to improve and expand your speaking skills because even if you've written the world's greatest keynote speech, you'll want to have built up your confidence enough to step onto the stage and deliver it with style, flair, and skill.

Name recognition is something we all work towards. It's one of the main reasons I put so much emphasis on developing speaking skills. One of your goals should always be to bring your best to the stage. When you do, every audience you stand in front of will leave feeling like they just participated in something special or meaningful. The reason you want to work with this goal in mind is because they *will* remember you; that's not the issue. It's how they will remember you that matters.

I received a call a few years ago from an out-of-state conference planner inquiring about my availability and fees to speak at a conference. (I just love it when I get those serendipitous calls from all over the country.) When I asked the gracious caller how she had heard about me, she said that she had been on a conference planning committee several years ago and had heard me speak. Since then, she had moved to another state, joined the regional state conference planning committee there, and was thrilled to be able to recommend me! This is the magic that comes from being prepared, skilled, seen, and heard.

Marketing Yourself to Those Who Don't Know You

While there are many conference planners that have heard of me, there are still many more that haven't. To change that, one of my speaking business tasks is to continue my search for potential clients. One of my internet searches found a potential client with a national presence. They had regional chapters in nearly every state; some states with multiple chapters, and each chapter with their own website. The best part was that nearly eighty percent of these chapters had conferences listed on their website. This equated to hundreds of potential conference planners in search of keynote speakers like me!

My next step was to contact each chapter via the contact information provided on their website to request the contact information of the person responsible for collecting information about potential keynote speakers. Once I knew who to send it to, I put a marketing/press kit together and mailed it out.

It was taking me a significant amount of time to send out email queries, make phone calls, play phone tag, package up my MPKs, and then take a trip to the post office, but I was determined to stick with it. This kind of long distance networking is crucial to my business as a keynote speaker.

I didn't do it for very long though. Instead, I took my own advice and hired someone to do the job for me. I found a young woman with prior experience working in a call center. She was a stay-at-home mom and her husband was currently deployed overseas. It was a perfect fit! I showed her how to do everything, arranged for her to work out of my home office a few days a week, and then let her take over.

She did an excellent job of digging through the chapter websites for contact information and then making phone calls or sending emails until she found the right person to mail the MPK to. Thanks to all her hard work, I now have a data base filled with potential clients, all their contact information, and a time table of when to reach out to them.

Between paying my assistant, putting together the MPKs, and paying postage, I spent a fair amount of money. But I knew that it was an investment in my speaking business, and it was worth every penny of it to get my speaker one-sheet into the hands of the people with the power to make a decision.

This is a perfect example of targeted marketing - a much more cost and time effective approach than blind marketing. It may take a little time to pay off because conference committees sometimes map out their conferences years in advance, but that won't matter once you're on their 'radar.' All you have to do from that point forward is to reach out to their contact person at regular intervals and keep them updated with your growing list of successes and recommendations.

Give Them Breakouts

Like anyone else with a budget, conference planners love to get as much as they can out of their keynote speaker. Sometimes they will ask the speaker they've hired to do a breakout workshop – or two – to further justify the keynote fees they will be paying. This is especially true when the speaker does a great job of inspiring, entertaining, and educating their audience.

Because the speaker's goal is to speak again, they're very likely to say yes to the request. Some keynote speakers take it a step further and add one or more breakout/workshop sessions at no additional charge when they submit their proposal. I always offer two additional breakouts as part of my keynote proposals to sweeten the deal - you should too!

What to Charge

The topic of determining your fee is always a tough one, especially when you're just getting started. To further complicate things, fees will vary between the different types of conferences and level of notoriety between the speakers. The fee that might be budgeted for a keynote speaker at a conference about the struggles people face when trying to maintain a healthy weight throughout their lifetime might be dramatically different than the fee budgeted for the keynote speaker at a conference focused on global warming. Each field of interest has its own range of fees and can be anywhere from $0 to over $100,000! Who could possibly get $100,000 for a 90 minute speech? Former president Bill Clinton for one.

The thing is, you don't have to have a goal of becoming a six figure keynote speaker. Your goal should be to become a respected and recommended speaker in the topic that you are both knowledgeable and passionate about. When you become that go-to speaker in your field, you'll start getting your keynote opportunities. I don't know what the fee range will be in your field, but I can suggest that if you're afraid you might be charging too much, you can always let the conference committee know that there might be some room to negotiate. For now, do some internet research to see what you can find out about what other keynotes in your field might be charging.

My typical clients are social service agencies, school systems and child care associations. I've found that they usually pay between $500 and $5000, depending on whether or not they've secured a grant. I give them my price but add "If this doesn't fit your budget, please contact me and let's see if we can find a way to work together so I can help you make your conference a huge success."

I've had conference planners openly express their appreciation for my willingness to be flexible. Some committees will access other budget line items to make up the difference. One conference made up the difference in the fee by accessing their book budget. With those funds they purchased a large inventory of my books so they could give one to everyone attending the conference.

Together, the money they paid for the books and the amount they paid me to speak, equaled the fee I had requested. And, I was basically able to sell everyone a copy of my book rather than having to set up a table at the back to sell a smaller number of books. I had a lot of books to sign as a result, but it was a good problem to have.

While any keynote speaker will tell you that it's important to stick to your speaking fee so that you don't become devalued by future clients, it's equally important to take all things into consideration before declining a lower offer. Consider other factors such as the length of time you are being asked to speak for, the distance and time it will take you to travel to the conference location, whether the client is paying for travel - or not, and even whether they will allow you to sell your products at the back of the room or at a vendor table. If the number isn't too far off from your set fee, consider accepting it.

Other times your fee will be accepted without any negotiations. I've had clients pay me my set fee plus all of my travel expenses, allow me to set up my back-of-the-room sales table, and then offer me a table in the vendor area at a discount.

One of those clients wanted me back the following year, but indicated that their budget had been significantly reduced. They had already decided on their keynote speaker, but wanted me to speak as one of their featured speakers. The fee they were offering was less than my normal speaking fee. After some negotiation though, they agreed to pay all of my travel expenses including extra nights in a plush hotel, and to provide me with a vendor table at no extra charge.

I accepted their offer because of my previous experience with them. I also wanted to stay on their short-list of candidates for another keynote opportunity. My family and I were able to enjoy some quality time away from home, and I was able to work the conference and clear nearly $2000 in book and CD sales at my vendor table.

Working with Speakers Bureaus

Professional keynote speakers are busy people. We spend our time updating our websites, blogs, social media connections, writing our next book, traveling, networking, and speaking. The one thing we don't have a lot of time for is marketing our speaking business. That's where speakers bureaus come in. They are booking agencies that market and sell keynote speaker services to organizations planning conferences.

Speaker's bureaus like clients with a minimum speaking fee of $5000. They will expect to see a top-notch marketing/press kit along with a substantial list of past speaking accomplishments. Although some will accept speakers simply because of their notoriety, bureaus will still be looking for extensive field experience and a solid working knowledge of their chosen topic.

You can find speakers bureaus by doing an internet search. On the bureau websites, check for speakers in your topic. Read the marketing material they use on the bureau site, and then go and check out their speaking business websites too. When you do this, you're going to see things you like and things you don't like. Then, you can use your impressions of their information to help you design, develop, and update your own speaker business image.

Zero Limits

All these keynote tasks may seem a little daunting right now, but again, becoming a keynote speaker doesn't have to be your main goal. The whole point of explaining what they are and how to get yourself positioned as a viable candidate is to show you that there aren't any upper limits when it comes to your speaking business. Knowing how to position yourself for keynote opportunities will help you come across as a true professional even if the opportunities you desire most are in your own hometown.

Now might be a good time to revisit Chapter 13 to remind yourself of how to start getting hired for those first conference bookings. Once your performance evaluations start generating high marks, the word will get around and you will end up getting calls from conference planners. When you feel confident enough to stand on that keynote stage, the strategies in this chapter will help you stand out as a candidate.

Commit to doing extensive searches for organizations, companies, and businesses related to your topic. This is when the internet is indispensable; it gives you access to global information. I know of two young men who have their brick and mortar business in their hometown, but they have been offered and accepted speaking opportunities in both Europe and Asia; and yes, their travel expenses were covered.

Find local conferences in your topic area and sit in the keynote audience. Attend that speaker's breakout sessions if they have them. Make notes about their presentation style, their format, and anything else you found interesting. Every piece of information you collect is another opportunity for you to improve your own speaking skills.

Chapter 21

Making Connections

People thrive when the connections they establish with other people are genuine, sincere, and supportive. When you're on stage, the goal of your connection with your audience isn't necessarily to be invited to dinner (although the occasional invitation is appreciated), it's to make a connection that allows you to share your message with an audience open to receiving it.

When you've successfully connected via the quality of your presentation, everyone in your audience is now a potential client. Some will be interested in your products and services for themselves, others will know someone they think you should meet. Outside of the workshop you'll be making connections with other speakers, event coordinators, staff, vendors, etc. In fact, every person you make contact with at the event is a potential client.

Before you decide on a strategy for taking advantage of all these contact opportunities during the event, you'll first need to find out if the conference has any restrictions when it comes to collecting information from attendees. Implementing your strategy without their permission is one sure way to never be invited back. Once you know it's okay to gather attendees contact information, it's time to choose your strategies for collecting.

The days of people freely offering up their personal information are gone. It's been replaced with reminders to protect your personal data and warnings to be suspicious of requests for it. That means that providing an index card and asking for a name, address, phone number, cell number and email address isn't likely to go over very well even if the conference is okay with it.

When you think about it, what information do you really need? Any person who really wants to talk to you is going to give you their phone number or business card, or ask for your business card so they can contact you. The information you are hoping to collect will give you access to your *future* potential clients, the people who want to know you better before making any decisions about doing business with you.

The single most effective piece of contact information you can collect from people is their email address. You can always give them the option of providing more, but email is the most efficient and cost effective way to stay connected with people interested in you and your content.

When you are scheduled to speak at an event, you can use a variety of techniques to encourage people to share their contact information with you.

- Let people know you have a newsletter you send out via email and have a sign-up sheet prepared to collect their names and email addresses.
- If you have a table in the vendor area, host a drawing for some of your products. Provide people with precut, preprinted (if it fits in your budget) slips of paper to write their name and email address on and a nice container to collect them in.
- If you have a sales table set up at the back of the room, have a giveaway planned at the conclusion of your presentation. Have someone let participants know about the giveaway as they are walking in so they can fill out their entry slips ahead of time rather than waiting until the very end.

One of my favorite things to do at the conclusion of a

presentation is to give away signed copies of my books and CDs. Yes, they have to give me their name and email address for a chance to win, but by now, these folks have seen me present and would love to walk away with any one of my products free of charge. They are also happy with the prospect of staying connected and getting more information related to what they learned that day.

Before I let them leave the room, I collect all the slips in a decorative bag and pull out the winners' names. They come up front and collect their prizes. It's also a great way to talk about my products without selling them! When I get home, I take the contact information I collected in the bag of entry slips, the email newsletter sign-up sheet, and the business cards I've collected and enter them into the email database I use to stay connected with my 'peeps.'

Now that you know some ways to start building your contact email database, you can start thinking about how you are going to stay in contact with them. There are so many strategies with this piece of the puzzle, too many to cover in this book.

As your list grows, you'll want to start thinking about using some type of email service. They can help you organize your email data, categorize your contact lists, create communication documents like emails and newsletters, set up auto email campaigns, and email them all out through spam-safe filters. Some of the top companies include: ConstantContact.com, GetResponse.com, MailChimp.com, GoDaddy.com, and AWeber.com.

Some of these companies charge a fee for their service and some offer a free option for smaller email lists. Even though you're just getting started, you'll want to take a look at them and consider the advantages of using them. Most of them provide easy-to-use newsletter creators that offer editable templates you can use to easily design informative newsletters to send out to your mailing list. Their templates are designed to be spam-safe and always provide the information required by law to give the recipient the ability to unsubscribe anytime they choose. Check out the email marketing companies I listed above and take a look at some of their self-guided tutorials.

Chapter 22

Wrapping Up the Event

This part of the book has covered a lot of territory and shared tools and techniques you can use to design a presentation that educates, inspires, and/or entertains your audience. If your objective is to educate, remember that people have different learning styles and preferences so include a variety of teaching methods to accommodate them.

Find ways to connect with your audience; when you do, they are much more likely to be inspired by the information you're sharing with them. And, if your objective is to entertain, adults love to laugh and have fun, so think of ways you can incorporate touches of humor into your presentation.

When you're event is over and you're home, there's one thing you'll want to do as soon as you can. Write down how the event went. This is for your personal benefit because unless you have a professional coach waiting at home, you're the one who's going to be reviewing the event and coming up with ways to grow and improve. Your event review should cover things like:

- *Checklists*: Look at the checklists you used. Did they do a good job of helping you prepare? Did they cover everything you needed to do prior to the event? Was your list of things to pack accurate? If they need updating, set aside some time to update them within the next few days. (Checklists are covered in Chapter 29.)
- *Your presentation*: Think about your presentation; did it go according to plan? Do you feel like it needs some adjustments? Did it fit within the time parameters or does it need to be longer or shorter? How did your audience respond to your techniques and

the way you organized your material? Were your handouts effective?

- **Event contact and staff:** Think about your contact person for the event. How were they to deal with: pleasant, abrupt, stressed? Are there event personnel who stood out?
- **Best & Worst:** Write down your favorite part of the conference and then your least favorite part.
- **One thing I need to remember:** Decide if there's something specific about this event that you definitely want to remember for the next time.
- **Who do I need to contact ASAP:** What information did you receive from other people that you want to follow up on? Is there anyone you want to contact as soon as possible?
- **Email addresses:** How well did your email contact collection strategies work?
- **Article, book, ebook, blog post ideas:** Are there any potential articles, books or blog topics that came to mind throughout the course of the event?

This might seem like a lot of work, but taking the time to record it frees your mind from the pressure of trying to remember it all. Then, when it's time to think about contacting the conference for next year, all you have to do is read your notes.

By now you can see that there are many ways and opportunities for designing and building a presentation that reflects who you are, how passionate you are about your topic, and how to best present it in ways that will be meaningful and accessible to your audience. You also see that it almost doesn't matter whether you are planning a workshop or a keynote; they use the same basic tools and techniques. Sometimes you will make adjustments for the length of time you have, the size of your audience and the scope of your coverage, but they all start the same way – with you sharing your message from the stage.

Once again, 'begin with the end in mind' and your participants will leave your room ready to share their positive experience with others, some of whom will want to talk with you about speaking at their next event.

Section
IV

Chapter 23

Writing a Book

"You've got to have a book!" That's what a friend told me many years ago. When I asked her why, she told me that every successful speaker she's ever heard had their book for sale at the back of the room after they spoke. Her opinion was that books increase credibility. I wasn't sure what to think because I didn't know if I could write a book; I was a professional speaker, not a professional writer.

Still, she got me thinking about it and as I started to look around, I realized that many professional speakers had written and were selling their own nonfiction books. Every time I turned on the television, another author of a self-help book was being interviewed on some talk show. I became aware of notices in my local newspaper announcing book signings and readings down at my local library. My friend was absolutely right and I began reading everything I could find on becoming the published author of a nonfiction book.

In 2007, when I started thinking about writing a book, the general message for getting your book in print was less than inspiring. It sounded like the only way a book publisher would take on an unknown author was if that person was already famous as was the case with Barrack Obama's book, *The Audacity of Hope*. I knew he was a good speaker, but was he a writer too? I hadn't accomplished something amazing like climbing Mount Kilimanjaro and I didn't have a harrowing tale to tell. I was me, Parenting and Child Behavior expert, Bill Corbett.

But I kept reading and started finding a lot of information about self-publishing. I eventually found the book: Dan Poynter's *Self-Publishing Manual: How to Write, Print and Sell Your Own Book*. In it he writes:

The prestige enjoyed by the published author is unparalleled in our society. A book can bring recognition, wealth and acceleration in one's career... If you publish yourself, you'll make more money, get to press sooner and keep control of your book. You'll invest your time as well as your money, but the reward will be greater. (Poynter, 2007)

Prior to Dan's book I believed the only way to have a bookstore quality book published was to become a client with one of the big book publishing giants. But now I was reading about how to self-publish. It was an exciting idea, and I began researching and reading everything I could find on the subject of self-publishing so I could come up with a plan for publishing my own book.

Now, in 2014, the idea that a regular person can share their message by self-publishing their own book is a realistic and viable option. I now have my own publishing company and have experienced firsthand the way people tend to automatically accept me as an expert just because I have a book in print.

When I last checked, there were over 60 companies offering printing options to authors who've decided to self-publish. The cost of getting your book in print varies quite a bit, and I'm always asking other self-published authors who they've used. The online print company I decided to use is one that a lot of other authors use too, Amazon's self-publishing platform, CreateSpace.com.

As of this printing, there are no required set up fees and their online self-help system is incredibly helpful and easy to follow. Whenever I've had to call them, I've always gotten to speak with a real person and they've always been very helpful. I paid less than $50 to make my book available to an extensive list of book seller/distributors. The only other money I paid to them was for the proof copy they printed and mailed to me.

The process of writing my books has also enhanced my speaking skills, helped me come up with additional topics to speak about, and increased my conference revenue. But more importantly, it's also given my audience a way to take something meaningful home with them when they leave. Your book is a way to keep your audience inspired long after they've had the pleasure of hearing you speak in person.

How I Wrote My Book

The first step with self-publishing is, of course, to write the book. Just thinking about it was overwhelming for me though. I didn't know where or how to start, so I did some research on "how to write a book." Even that was a bit overwhelming and then I thought about something I teach in my parenting classes.

I tell parents to think about the different aspects of the chores they want their children to do from their child's perspective. To their young minds a task that seems simple to you, might be overwhelming simply because they don't know how or where to start. The fix for this situation is to break the chore down into smaller, more easily managed chunks. As each chunk is completed, their sense of accomplishment grows. Before they know it, the child has completed the chore and is less likely to be overwhelmed by the thought of doing it the next time it needs to be done. I know this works, so I applied the technique to my quest to write a book.

The first thing I did was to dust off a few of my freshman college books on how to write. Their advice was similar; break down the overall topic of the book into smaller, easier to write sections. As I was thinking about how to break my book into sections, I was also getting a better feel for what my book would be about and who my audience would be.

My expertise is in parenting, discipline and child behavior, so I thought about the parents and teachers who were my customers and then I thought about what I could offer them.

When I speak, the audience is always listening to what I have to say. Granted, it's because I know my topic and the stage very well, but I also think they are waiting to hear what I might have to say about a specific situation they are currently dealing with. I decided to make a list of the questions I typically heard at my lectures. The result of this effort was a list of 'The Top 10 Parenting Problems' that the parents I met were struggling with.

Another piece of advice I had read numerous times was *Don't Start at Chapter 1*! I understood the logic of this idea. It's nonfiction, so it's not like I have to start at the beginning. Instead I could start with whichever one of the 10 questions I was drawn to write about first. It worked. I picked the one that I knew the most about and began to write. I would spend a little bit of time working on it every day. Within two weeks time, I had written about 1000 words.

This process went on for a few months. Along the way, I had to learn how to deal with all the new chapter topics that kept popping into my head while I was trying to write about the topics I had already decided on. I tried jotting those ideas down on a piece of paper so I could forget about them right now and stay focused on the writing in front of me, but all those thoughts were starting to discourage me. Each new chapter idea piled onto the list of all the other things I felt like I had to do before I would be able to publish my book.

One of the major differences between speaking on stage and writing a book is that with speaking you have a topic, and even though you are always improving your presentations, they still have a beginning, a middle, and an end; all of which occur in an average of 90 minutes. I was getting discouraged and a bit overwhelmed because I couldn't predict how much time it was going to take to finish it; I didn't have anything to compare it with.

Couple those thoughts with all the discouraging comments I had received from family members who had gone out of their way to try and convince me that no one in our family would ever make a living by speaking, and certainly not by writing books, and you have a clear picture of how one task might turn into the challenge of a lifetime.

I just kept reminding myself of the delight I would feel when I held that book in my hands. I knew I was writing something that would help people – real people and no matter how many stages I was able to stand on, I wasn't going to have access to all the people who could benefit from this information. A book, my book, had the potential of reaching and helping so many other people. With those thoughts in mind, I pushed on.

I disciplined myself to remain focused only on that one chapter I was working on at that moment. I would pretend that this chapter was the entire book and all I had to do was complete it to finish the book.

After writing in every spare moment of time that I had for nearly five months, the manuscript was completed. I hired someone to edit it and bartered with a graphics designer to create the cover. Within just a couple of weeks of finishing the manuscript and uploading it to CreateSpace.com, I was holding the proof copy of my first book in my hands. It was a day I will always remember.

After taking some time to let it sink in that I had actually written a book, I reread the book and examined it from cover to cover. I went online to fix things that needed fixing and in less than two weeks UPS delivered the first case of my new book. At my next conference, it felt great to have a table at the back of the room where people could purchase a copy of my brand new book! Signing those first books was an experience I'll never forget!

About a year after publishing my first book, I was doing a lecture and book signing at a local school. To my surprise, one of my brothers and his fiancée showed up and took a seat in the audience. I never expected to see him (or anyone else from my family for that matter) at one of my events. I only had a couple of minutes before I was supposed to start, but I grabbed a book off of my sales table and headed over to them. I greeted them, signed the book, gave it to him, and then headed to the front of the room to begin my lecture.

At the end of the presentation, a line of people formed by the stage with both parenting questions and copies of my book for me to sign. At the end of the line were my brother and my soon-to-be sister-in-law. When they finally got their turn and approached me, my brother said "You were great. It's hard to believe that someone from our family is capable of standing on a stage and teaching a whole room full of people. And, you wrote a book! Very impressive."

I hope reading about my first experience with writing a book doesn't discourage you from writing yours. I related the story above to encourage you and to let you know that even things that aren't easy to do, can be done. Feeling discouraged or overwhelmed is often a side effect of trying new things. If writing is easy for you, then it might be some other part of the process that challenges you and generates those feelings.

The point is that you get to choose what you want to focus on. Don't let any of that junk that pops into your mind, or any of those negative comments casually tossed your way, impose their agenda on you. Stay focused on your message and how your message is going to help people. Imagine what it's going to feel like when you are holding *your* book in your hands.

If you're just getting started, you may be too busy to add 'writing a book' to your to-do list. But at some point in your speaking career you're going to be ready to write your book. For now, while you're creating all your outlines and organizing your ideas for your presentations, start a file folder for any thoughts or ideas you have for your first (or your next) book. You might also consider doing a little research about the process of self-publishing. I've learned a lot from Dan Poynter's *Self-Publishing Manual: How to Write, Print and Sell Your Own Book*. He offers excellent advice and great insights throughout his book; a lot of which I followed:

If you can voice an opinion and think logically, you can write a book. If you can *say it*, you can *write it*. Most people have to work for a living and therefore can spend only a few minutes of each day on their book. Consequently, they can't keep the whole manuscript in their head. They become overwhelmed and confused, and find it easy to quit the project. The solution is to break up the manuscript into many small, easy-to-attack chunks (and never start at page one, where the hill looks steepest). Then concentrate on one section at a time and do a thorough job on each part.

People want to know "how to" and "where to," and they will pay well to find out. The information industry... now amounts to more than one-half of the U.S. gross national product. There is money in information. (Poynter, 2007)

If you believe that your expertise as a speaker helps people live better and happier lives, or teaches them how to do something better, then you have a book in you. In Marc McCutcheon's book *Damn! Why Didn't I Write That!* he says:

People need nonfiction books. They need reference books, how-to guides, self-help tomes, histories, directories, cookbooks, travelogues, chronicles, manuals... They need to know how to make more money. They need to know how to keep themselves healthy. They need to know more about current events and world affairs. They need to know how to run their computers, repair leaky faucets, and trim their butts and bellies. They need to stay abreast of trends, rip-offs, corruption, scandals, politics, crime, education, careers, scientific breakthroughs... the list goes on and on. In short, they need a galaxy of useful, practical titles. Not only do they need these titles, they will often pay a premium for them if they think they can find the information no place else. (McCutcheon, 2006)

Chapter 24

How to Write an eBook without Typing a Word

Even though we covered how writing a book can increase your credibility and your status as a professional speaker, I can understand how the thought of writing a whole book and then taking it through the whole publishing process might be a bit overwhelming right now. But, what if you could write a book without typing one word? Well, thanks to the wonders of technology you can. It's called an ebook.

An eBook is your book in a digital form that can be purchased online and downloaded to a computer, a laptop, and a variety of other internet capable devices. There are a lot of advantages to eBooks. For one thing, eBooks don't have to be as expansive as books in print. In fact, there are people who prefer getting their information in smaller quantities; it's easier to absorb. Here is what professional speaker and author Marc Ostrofsky says in the book *Get Rich CLICK: The Ultimate Guide to Making Money on the Internet*:

> EBooks – electronic books – are becoming increasingly popular, especially with the advent of Amazon's Kindle... Kindle owners can shop for books on Amazon and download them without access to a computer. Amazon has managed to create an impressive library, and it is now evident that the Kindle, the Nook, the iPad and other similar devices will transform the entire publishing industry forever.
>
> Knowing this to be a certainty, think what opportunities are being created due to this huge industry shift. There are so many changes that are taking place now – basically anything and everything is about

to change in the publishing world. Even the term BOOKS. If in the future, physical books are a rarity and eBooks are the wave of the future, will our children be telling their friends it's a good book or a good read? (Ostrofsky, 2012)

Let me ask you again, would you consider writing a book if you didn't have to type one word? Think about it, no typing at all and you can still have an eBook to sell. Let me tell you how it can be done.

Your Content

Let's say you're an expert with selling mattresses. You started your career working at one of the major mattress retailers; maybe you like it so much you still work there. Through the years, you've built up an impressive body of knowledge about healthy sleep habits and how much of an impact the type of mattress you sleep on can have on your ability to enjoy a good night's sleep.

You've launched your new speaking business and have been giving lectures to the public on how to get a better night's sleep. Customers tell the sales people in all those other mattress stores that they heard you speak and realized they needed a new mattress. The managers in those stores now want to hire you to come in and do some sales training with their staff because you clearly know how to sell a mattress.

Up until this point, every time someone says, "You should write a book!" you've dismissed the idea because you don't think of yourself as a writer. But today someone explained how to write an eBook without typing one word. Your response now? "Let's write an eBook!"

In chapter 8, we talked about all the ways a digital recorder can be used to help you create content. Now, we're going to add writing an eBook to the list of ways you can use your digital recordings.

When it comes to the talks about mattresses, there are two potential audiences: an audience of mattress customers and an audience of mattress sales people. Both of these audiences would be interested in an eBook. Make a recording of each of one your talks. You can wait until you're scheduled to speak again and tape your presentation while you're giving it, or you can choose not to wait until your next scheduled presentation and instead, record the presentation while sitting comfortably at home. Once you have your recordings, you'll want to download them to your computer using the cable that came with the digital recorder.

The next step is to have someone transcribe one of the recordings into text. There are a number of ways to get this done and by the time you're reading this book, there may be several more! Here are two of the ways you can get a recording transcribed today:

Do it Yourself: There are programs you can download to your computer that will slow a recording down to a rate where you can easily type your lecture into a text document. One software package I have used personally is called TRANSCRIBE! and you can find it at SeventhString.com. It sells for about $40 and is very easy to use.

Hire a Transcriber: Once again, this is a great time to head over to Fiverr.com where you will find hundreds of people willing to transcribe up to 10 minutes of an audio file for just $5. If your lecture is 30 minutes long, it will cost you $15. If your lecture is an hour, you'll pay just $30 for the whole recording to be transcribed. That's one heck of deal; and, as promised, you didn't need to type one word!

Once your lecture is in a text format, you're going to need

someone with editing skills to edit your text. Even if it looks good to you as it is right now, this is a step you don't want to skip. A good editor will enhance your prose and improve your product; they will fix all those pesky punctuation problems and in the end, those edits can translate into dollars, referrals and more speaking opportunities. And, your eBook will look and read like the work of a professional writer.

If you don't have anyone in your personal network with editing skills, once again you can turn to Fiverr.com where there are plenty of eager editors ready to edit your document of up to 500 words for just $5.

The Cover

EBooks don't require a fancy cover, but a book's cover can sometimes influence a person's decision when it comes to buying, so you'll still want to make sure that yours looks professional. You might even already have an idea for your cover; all you need is someone to do the actual computer work. Think about your network again. Do you know anyone with graphic design experience? If you don't, do a few internet searches for book covers to see who's offering their online services. And yes, check out Fiverr.com.

Almost There!

Once you've gone through the steps of recording, transcribing, editing, adding a cover, and then saving your eBook as a word document, it's ready to be turned into the computer friendly format called a PDF. Some versions of Microsoft Word will allow users to save their documents as PDFs. To find out if your version of Word will allow you, open your document and select the 'save as' option. If PDF doesn't show up as a format option, then you won't be able to convert it directly from your word processing program.

One way to solve this problem is to download a free PDF

converter program that will add a PDF converter to the printer options on your computer. Once installed, whenever you want to save a document as a PDF, hit the print command, go to the drop-down box where you can select a printer and you'll see the PDF option. Click on the PDF option, then click okay, and the program will save your document as a PDF. There are many versions of this free software. To find one, go to www.cnet.com and type 'free PDF converter' into their search box.

Now that you have your book saved as a word document and as a PDF, you're also going to want to create a secured PDF. This is the copy you can send out to people in your professional network for feedback, comments and endorsements. Sending a secure PDF ensures that no one can make changes or edits without your permission.

A well known software used to accomplish this task is Adobe Acrobat. Most people have Adobe Acrobat *Reader* on their computer so they can open and read PDFs, but the PDF reader is not the same thing as the pricey Adobe Acrobat software. Fortunately, you don't need to worry about forking out your hard earned cash to secure your PDF.

Think about your network first. Do you know anyone who has Adobe Acrobat that might be willing to lock the document for you? It takes about one minute to do and anybody with the full Adobe Acrobat program can do it. If that's not an option, there are websites you can use to secure your PDF. A lot of them are free, but you'll need to check their file size limit first. There are also subscription services where you pay a small monthly fee for the privilege of creating and securing as many PDFs as you want. And, if all else fails, you can always go to Fiverr.com.

After following these steps, you should have your completed eBook on your computer; it has a cover and is saved as a word document, a regular PDF and a secured/locked PDF. Congratulations! The last step is to get it online for sale.

Selling Your eBook

There are a lot of ways to get your eBook online. Some require more work than others because different services have their own unique formatting requirements. The website I'm going to talk about here is SmashWords.com. It's free to sign up, and they will walk you through the process of uploading your word document. They do the formatting work and then put your eBook for sale on their digital shelf.

Smashwords.com is also an authorized eBook distributor for most major online eBook retailers. They charge a modest fee for this service, and you can find the list of retailers they distribute to on their website. If you take advantage of their distribution services, your eBook will be made available across a variety of retailers and platforms so that it can be downloaded to a long list of devices including: electronic eBook readers, personal computers, iPad, iPhone, iPod Touch, the Kindle, Kindle Fire, Sony Reader, Barnes & Noble's Nook, etc.

Ready to Start Writing?

As promised, you now have a whole eBook without having had to type one word! You also know at least one website where you can put it up for sale. If you're still on the fence about whether or not to create an eBook, Marc Ostrofsky has some thoughts to share on the subject in his book *Get Rich CLICK*:

10 Reasons Why eBooks Can Help You Make Money and Save You Money:

1. EBooks are CONSIDERABLY less expensive to publish and distribute than physical books.
2. Many eBooks are available online as free downloads, as samples, marketing hooks or bonuses.
3. EBooks are easier than traditional books to produce. The author or publisher creates the electronic book

once and sells the same digital file over and over and over.

4. There are no printing or binding costs.
5. Because the product is delivered electronically online, there are no shipping, distribution or book warehousing costs.
6. Reselling the rights to an eBook can encourage a viral effect.
7. EBooks can be revised easily.
8. Your target market may prefer reading online. EBook customers often prefer convenient desktop viewing.
9. Delivery of an electronically downloaded book on a Kindle is virtually instantaneous, which satisfies those who want their content now.
10. The up-front costs are the same whether you sell the eBook to one person or one million people. (Ostrofsky, 2012)

Chapter 25

Selling Your Audio and Video Products

Nowadays there are more ways than ever to sell your content both off and online. In one sense, it might be hard to think of your message - something that you're very passionate about – and the whole idea of *selling* it. What you want to remember is that every format and purchase option you provide increases the chances of someone finding and benefitting from a collection of ideas, information, knowledge, solutions and/or strategies they've been hoping to find.

People are even more excited when the information is provided in a variety of formats because then it can be easier for them to fit it into their lifestyle. So far, we have talked about a couple of different ways to use your digital recordings. The next logical option is to create a CD.

There are a lot of advantages to CDs. People can listen to them just about anywhere. They can listen to them in their cars, in their homes, and if they know how, they can download them to their computers and then upload them to MP3 players. CDs are a physical product that people can hold in their hands as well as being an excellent addition to your back-of-the-room sales table.

By now, your technical knowledge and/or skills are growing, but as we continue to cover new applications, remember that the internet is loaded with help. If you aren't sure about how to do something, do searches both on the internet and at YouTube.com. Each will offer up a variety of answers and how-to information for the simplest to the most complex of your questions.

Editing Your New Audio Product

We already talked about how to download your recordings onto your computer. We already covered Audacity.com as a free program that will help you edit your recordings. The best thing about having learned how to do all these things is that now you don't have to pay someone else to do them for you! All these new technologies really do put the ability to create a quality CD in your hands.

As you begin the process of creating your CD, you're going to want to sit down and really listen to your recordings. One thing you will be listening for is things you'd like to edit *out* of the recording like: specific words or sentences, coughing, clearing your throat, sneezes, or long pauses.

You will also be listening for opportunities to add things like: an introduction, a conclusion, a biography, or information about how to contact you. Before you start adding content though, do an internet search about how to make your recordings sound more professional and set up your own little recording comfort zone. From there, you can record or re-record material for your CDs.

The only serious limit with a CD is time; if your recoding is too long, you will need to edit it so that it fits within the 80 minute time limit of a typical CD. If your recording is a lot less than 80 minutes, you can edit in bonus content at the end - like one of your podcasts. In fact, you could create a whole CD using a few of your podcasts with an introduction edited in before each one.

Also consider breaking your recording into segments, like tracks on a music CD. They will allow for easy navigating when people want to rewind or fast forward your CD to hear your content again.

Adding Music and Sound Effects to Your Production

There are many options when it comes to enhancing the quality of your CDs, music being one of the most impressive. Fortunately, you don't have to worry about composing or playing the music because there is music available on the internet.

Royalty free music is music uploaded to the internet by a composer, musician, and/or publisher for you to use. If you do an internet search for the words 'royalty free music' you will turn up hundreds of options. These websites are like online music shops and will charge a small fee for the download, but it's a one-time fee and there won't be any additional expenses or royalty fees expected at a later date.

While you're checking out the royalty free music, check to see if they offer sound effects too. Granted, sound effects might not be appropriate for all your content, but you never know. You might hear something that you'd never have thought about adding to your recordings until you've heard it.

Whether you decide to add content, music, and/or sound effects to your CD, be patient and give yourself the time to learn how to do it. Remember, most programs come with help files, and whatever you can't find there is probably available on the internet or at YouTube.com.

Getting Your CD Ready for Its Debut

One of the reasons you create a CD is to have another way for your audience to take something memorable home with them after hearing you speak. It's also another product you can add to your back-of-the-room sales table. You can sell it independently of your book and sign it just like you would your book, or you can offer a special price for people who decide to purchase both your book and your CD.

Any way you look at it, it's another opportunity to make an impression with the quality of your work. The next question is: who's going to make the CDs? You're first option, is to do the work yourself. If you choose this route, you will need a computer with an internal or external DVD drive with burn capabilities (the ability to copy and transfer media files from your computer), and some blank CDs. Most computers already come with some type of media program that will allow you to burn your content onto a CD.

After burning the CDs, you'll want to add some type of label. It doesn't need to be fancy, but you do want the front of the CD to have some information on it so that people will be able to look at it and know what's on it.

One low tech solution is to handprint the label. Maybe you know someone with excellent handwriting or calligraphy skills who can add the CD information by hand. If you are thinking about burning a lot of CDs, another option is to use a CD face label software.

I have used a label maker software program that I found at Acoustica.com with great success. As of today, you can download it for around $22 and use their extensive collection of templates to design and print everything you need for the CD and the CD case.

Once you have your CD, your two best options for protecting it are a sturdy paper CD sleeve or a harder plastic CD case, both available in bulk online or at your local office supply store. The only thing the CD you produce won't have is the cellophane wrapping. If you decide you want that type of professional seal, you'll have to consider getting your CD professionally duplicated.

Fortunately, in the same way that there are many self-publishing companies ready to help you with your book, there are also many CD self-publishing companies ready to help you with your CD.

It's an option to seriously consider because at some point

you might be too busy to do all the work yourself. Most online CD self-publishing businesses work the same way that the book ones do. You upload your content - your edited recording, cover(s), label and liner notes - and then let them do the work of putting it all together. Some online companies even have their own eStores so you can list and start selling your CD almost immediately. Two websites you can visit for more information about self-publishing your CD are www.CDBaby.com and www.CreateSpace.com.

When I started to look into the options of having someone make the CDs for me, I was a little concerned about how much it would cost. The prices weren't bad at all though, and the per CD price went down as the quantity ordered went up. I paid a small fee to a friend for help with designing the front and back covers, the inside liner notes, and the CD face label.

I decided to use CreateSpace to sell and distribute my CDs because I had set up an account with them when I self-published my first book. Once the CD project was completed, uploaded and approved, I ordered the first batch for less than $5 each and within 2 weeks I was holding my first CD in my hand. Because I had used CreateSpace.com, my CDs were also automatically released for sale on Amazon too!

Producing and Publishing Videos and DVDs

Now that we've covered most of the written and audio possibilities, there's only one other medium to cover – video. Here too, the opportunities are just about as endless as they are with books, ebooks, podcasts and CDs. If you decide you'd like to make your material available as a DVD, many self-publishing companies - both off and online - offer services that will help you turn your video recording into a physical product.

There are many ways to record your video. Most new computers come with some type of video editing software that will allow you to create and edit your own movies and/or create multimedia presentations. Devices that will record motion come in so many shapes and sizes that there's no possible way to list them all. Even if I could, someone is very likely to add a new device tomorrow.

As I write this, there is a new product at Swivl.com that allows iPhone users to capture both video and audio using a rotating docking station and a marker. The speaker wears the marker and the docking station swivels to track and record video while following the marker. The good news is that this tech savvy recording option is priced under $200 - as long as you provide the iPhone.

Having videos available will help increase your credibility and provide you with more opportunities to market yourself. If you haven't explored YouTube yet, go to www.YouTube.com and check it out. It's probably one of the most popular video posting websites on the internet, and it has every kind of video you can imagine posted there. There are many other websites offering the same upload and post format for video content. One nice thing is that you can have your video content on more than one website at a time. Just make sure to read each website's details and disclaimers before you upload.

For a speaker, video clips are an excellent way to let people see you 'in action.' After you make a video recording of one of your presentations, you can also edit it to create video clips to post online. Once you've uploaded the video, you can add the link to your online marketing/press kit so that the event planners who find you can see how well you handle the stage. You can also let everyone in your online and social media community know about it and invite them to view it by posting a link for them to click on.

Again, there are many options for you to explore and the technology available today is so amazing that sometimes it's a challenge not to be overwhelmed by all the possibilities these new options present. But having the technology available today doesn't mean you have to start today.

When you are ready to start creating products, there's likely to be new and improved technology to help you create them better and faster. On the other hand, if you feel like you're ready to start building your product line right now, there are many professionals ready, willing, and able to help you create your content and turn it into a variety of products quicker.

Making the Most of Your Products

One of the great things about all this technology is that you can create a product today, upload it to the internet today, and then it's available 24/7, 365 days a year, just waiting to be found and purchased by people who hear about you, see you speak, stumble onto your website or social media posts, or are referred by someone else. I've even had conference planners purchase digital products to experience my material before making the decision to hire me.

To be clear, I'm not saying you should sit down and try to create a product in one day; even a seasoned veteran will tell you that it takes time to produce quality products. At some point though, you'll want to become familiar with the different possibilities. The whole subject of which internet services to use, and the pros and cons of physical versus digital products, is another topic that's just too expansive to cover in this book. As your knowledge and comfort level with creating your products and utilizing the internet as part of your marketing/sales strategy grows, these are options to explore:

Fulfillment houses can help you with your physical products. You set up an account with them and then when people order your physical products, the fulfillment house sends it to the customer. Some houses will have your products on hand; some will 'print on demand.' Either way, when you use their services, you won't have to take any time out of your schedule to get your physical products into your customer's hand.

Online Marketplaces like ClickBank.com and Pay-Loads.com are online stores set up to deliver your products digitally. When people visit those sites they can search for you by name or find you as the result of a search they perform in their area of interest. Using a service like this also makes it easier for people who hear about your products in your emails, newsletters, ebooks, on your website, etc., to buy them just by clicking the link you've provided. They click, complete the transaction, and the product is available almost immediately.

The great thing about digital delivery is that it provides instant gratification for your customers; just a few clicks and they have it. The other great thing about digital products is that they work for you while you sleep. I love waking up to emails notifying me of products people purchased while I was enjoying a good night's sleep. It's a great way to start the day.

The only limits with the internet... well, there don't really seem to be any limits with the internet. Reach out to other professionals you know who have products for sale online and ask them how they handle this piece of the puzzle. Every day, someone turns something they've dreamed of into a reality. The smart ones figure out how to use the internet to get the word out.

Section

V

Chapter 26

Using Humor and Keeping It Original

One of the greatest rewards for a stage speaker is to hear an audience break out into laughter in response to something intentionally meant to be funny. Their laughter is great because it helps them relax and enjoy your presentation more. Every speaker who uses humor does it in their own unique way like the speaker who used the plastic milk crate, or the one who handed out the red clown noses. Even the most solemn of occasions might benefit from the inclusion of a touch of tasteful humor. The overall result of bringing humor into a presentation is a more enjoyable experience and a greater likelihood of both your content and your skill being remembered.

In some of my presentations I unveil a rusty, old, banged-up toolbox. For the next 20 minutes I pull a variety of objects out of the toolbox and use them as metaphors for how out-dated some of our ideas about parenting can be. One object is an enormous pair of glasses with large evil eyes attached. As I place the glasses on my face, I talk about one of the most common outdated tools – *the Death Stare* – and how we are ineffectively using it on our children to send them the message that they better behave NOW!

Hearty laughter explodes from my audience. They are laughing at my silly appearance on the stage, but they are also laughing at themselves for still using this age-old fear motivator to try and get their kids to behave. This antic is just one of several sight gags I use to get my audience to laugh at the difficult job we all have when it comes to parenting.

Humor can be a very personal response because different things are funny to different people. The one advantage with being a speaker is that you already know a lot about your audience; you know they are there to hear about something specific. When it comes to bringing humor onto the stage with you, the one piece of advice I can offer is to remember that the funniest things in life are very often the real things that happen to us and our circle of family, friends, and acquaintances. Be creative when it comes to sharing real life situations and the humor of it will come across in honest and true ways that your audience will relate to. The only caveat - change the names to protect the innocent!

When I was writing this book, I reached out to many of my fellow professional speakers and had the pleasure of talking with Darren LaCroix, the 2001 World Champion of Public Speaking. Darren and I both grew up in Massachusetts and attended Toastmasters chapters just 60 miles apart. He had posted a recent article on the topic of using humor in public speaking and the importance of using your own original content. After speaking with him, and with his permission, I have included his excellent advice for you here:

> In the mid 90's, I attended a speaker's conference in Nova Scotia. Still an amateur in comedy — and even greener in the speaker's world — I was excited to sit in on a breakout session on 'how to be funny' as a speaker. I had attended a few sessions in the past and found most of the

presenters to be funny, but not really explain the 'how' to be funny. It usually felt more like a chance for them to shine, rather than teach. This one sounded different — it was, after all, a regional conference, not a local event.

I was shocked! Absolutely beside myself — and me and myself were both ripping mad! The gist of the presenter's instructions was to find funny stories in old Reader's Digest magazines and memorize them! The presenter actually said, "If they are from years ago, people won't remember the stories."

My head exploded. "WHAT!?!" Not only is that stealing, but you'll never learn how to do it yourself with that strategy. I not only filled out the evaluation form, I filled out the whole backside of the paper as well. This event actually ignited my passion for teaching 'how to' workshops. It was what I craved and I saw very few other workshop leaders teaching a specific 'how to.' This is when I thought, "Not only is this wrong, but I can help people better than those presenters!" This incident also led me to making sure our Lady & the Champs Speaker's Conference is very content-rich.

You see, I grew up in the comedy world, where the fastest way to end a career was to use other comedian's material. It's a small world and everyone knows everyone else's lines, making it easy to spot those who steal. I've learned over the years that somehow people in the 'emerging speaker' world think it's OK to use lines that were written by another speaker. It isn't 'policed' as much in the speaking world as it is in comedy. I want you to know that it is not OK!

In the Boston comedy scene where I started, there were about fifty working comedians. In the emerging speaker market, there are literally tens of thousands around the world. As people go up in fees though, the numbers are dramatically reduced. Working speakers in the $5000-and-above fee range are a relatively small group. Event planners know other event planners and speakers in that range often share the stage with colleagues. They get to know each other's material and stories — and they talk.

A couple months after I gave my "Ouch!" speech at the National Speakers Association, Rick Segel and Larry Winget were speaking in the UK and witnessed someone there do 'my fall.' When they 'called' the speaker on it, he at first denied having seen me do it at the national convention, but later admitted that he was actually there.

Though that speaker may have gotten some compliments from others, what do you think happened to his credibility in the eyes of Rick and Larry? Do you think they'll ever refer him? It's a small world, especially at the top.

I've had a professional speaker, who should have known better, actually use a page from one of my handouts and teach humor from it! The shock was that it was at the same conference where I'd spoken the previous year. That's not OK! The speaker got a call from me and, to my surprise; they saw nothing wrong with what they'd done. Yikes!

They ignored the © at the bottom of the page. I may have expected it from a novice, but a pro? It's not OK!

Rory Vaden, when teaching his humor workshop, uses a couple of my ideas with my permission and gives me credit. That's perfect. That is OK!

Recently it came to my attention that someone from one of our Champ Camps had published an eBook. I had more than one person tell me that this speaker was teaching our material without giving proper credit. When I looked at it, though, there was some original information. It seemed to be a 'highlight reel' of teachings from other Champs, and me. The bigger challenge was that no credit was given. I emailed the person and they replied, telling me that they had "reworded" the content from their own head so they thought it was OK. Here's how they replied:

"Most of the techniques were known to speakers in ancient Greece, actors of the past, etc....For example many speakers of today use techniques taught by Dale Carnegie. Carnegie learned them from Socrates and Socrates learned them from somebody else."

That is absolutely correct. Universal principles can't have a copyright. Specific techniques and applications, however, can be copyrighted. For example, my message in my speech "Ouch!" is being willing to fail — a universal principle. I found out after winning that John Maxwell had a book titled *Failing Forward* — same universal principle.

What I saw in this eBook was some of our exact terminology. The speaker in my previous example, from the UK, who had 'lifted' my fall idea, learned (realized) the power of truth, brand, and credibility.

Much of what I teach has been learned from Patricia Fripp, Craig Valentine, and Lou Heckler — not to mention Mark Brown. Give credit. Make your material your own by personalizing it from your life experience. I remember seeing a speaker at a summer school class who gave a wonderful speech on self-responsibility. I was mesmerized. A few years later I heard Tony Robbins give the exact same example. Yikes. I hadn't realized that I'd seen a copy back in summer school because that was before I'd become aware of Tony and his material. At an amateur comedy night in Boston, I saw someone do a Robin Williams routine — word for word. He bombed. The truth will find a way.

Many professional speakers may have made a similar mistake early in their careers. Once you become aware, stop. I should thank the teachers who teach their students to steal material. They inspired me to become a teacher. I realized I could help people more than they were helping.

I'm grateful for my comedy upbringing, which taught me that although it's more work to create unique material, doing the work actually forces me to grow faster. It may seem like a shortcut to 'lift' someone else's material, but it lengthens the road to becoming a paid professional. It can be challenging when you get started. If it were easy, everyone would become a success. The audience wants to know your story from your experience.

Regurgitating someone's material, especially without giving credit... that's not OK!

In 1992 Darren LaCroix took the stage in a Boston comedy club and bombed miserably. It was horrible. The headliner that night told him to "keep his day job." Friends told him his dream was "crazy" & "stupid."

He didn't listen. He may have been "born without a funny bone in his body," but he possessed the desire to learn and the willingness to fail, all essential to achieving his dream. The self-proclaimed "student of comedy" is living proof that anything can be learned. When his high school English teacher found out he wrote a book, Laugh & Get Rich, she laughed.

Less than nine years later in 2001, Darren LaCroix out-spoke 25,000 contestants from 14 countries to become the World Champion of Public Speaking. He did it with a very funny speech. Now he inspires people to pursue and live their own dreams. He also helps guide emerging professional speakers to launch their careers in his Get Paid to Speak community. You can connect with him at www.GetPaidToSpeak.com.

Chapter 27

Event Etiquette

Etiquette is more than manners; it's also about expectations, an awareness of how to show respect for others, and sometimes more importantly – how to not look like an idiot. As speakers, we have at least one advantage; we know we're always going to be interacting with new people. The more people we 'meet and greet,' the more comfortable we become with the various social expectations people have when they meet us, which in turn helps us to make a better first impression.

When it comes to the rules of etiquette, there are too many to cover in just one chapter, but there is one rule worth emphasizing: always remember to say 'please' and 'thank you.' I've already talked about the importance of sending a thank you note after the event, but you will never run out of opportunities to say please and thank you during the course of an event.

Events often have a staff, sometimes an all volunteer staff. Either way, when you need something, figure out a way to get that 'please' into your request. After they've helped you, regardless of the outcome, take the few seconds it takes to express your gratitude for their help.

When you're addressing your audience, there will be times when please fits right in, like when you are asking them to turn off their cell phones. There's a big difference between saying "Remember to turn off your cell phones" and "If you could please turn your cell phones off, that would be great." A lot of speakers forget or neglect to figure out a way to thank their audiences for joining them on the journey between the beginning and the end of their presentation. When that happens, they've lost another opportunity to connect.

It's true that people won't always respond or acknowledge your social graces, but that's about them, not about you. Your decision and commitment to be respectful of others and to always make an effort to say please and thank you will circle back to you in truly good and unexpected ways.

Business Etiquette expert, Karen Thomas, has generously provided some of her advice when it comes to some of the etiquette challenges we face as speakers...

As an etiquette expert, I often find myself behind a lectern at colleges, universities, and in corporate meeting rooms on a weekly basis. This beautiful wooden device has almost become a second home to me, and I have to admit – I'm quite comfortable there. Maybe it's my Italian heritage that's at the core of my ability to comfortably speak to an audience of knowledge hungry listeners regardless of how large or small their numbers are.

Over the years, my experience as a speaker and corporate trainer has continued to reinforce the importance of the protocols I follow each and every time I speak. I don't think anyone who's sat in my audience has any doubt about how passionate I am when it comes to helping others grasp the advantage of having great social skills. For people who take the stage, knowing the intricacies of social etiquette before, during and after they speak can be crucial to their success.

Introductions are often over-looked because people "assume" they know how to perform. As a speaker though, you will be meeting a lot of people and shaking a lot of hands. Learning and mastering the art of the handshake - the tone of voice used, the stance, and making eye contact – will help you start out on the right foot, or hand! Here are the simple and easy to follow five S's I share with my audiences:

Stand– regardless of gender, when making or receiving an introduction, one must stand to greet the individual.

See – look the person directly in the eye; it shows your sincere interest.

Smile – always flash those pearly whites; it shows that you're "happy" to be meeting them.

Say – when you're introducing yourself, always use your first and last name. For example: "Hello, I am Dr. Jane Doe." Always use the other person's name when you are greeting them; for example: "It is very nice to meet you John, glad you could be with us today."

Shake – a firm grasp of the hand and a few good pumps; 2 to 3 are appropriate.

If you've ever wondered about how hard you should grip the hand of the person you are meeting, there is something called the "Toothpaste Test" that can help you get a grip on your grip. Open a full tube of toothpaste, grip it in the middle and proceed as if you are shaking someone's hand. If the toothpaste squirts out of the end of the tube into the sink, your grip is too harsh and should be loosened. If the paste doesn't even come close to the opening of the tube, then your handshake is too loose. If you are able to grip the tube and get the paste to appear at the end of the tube without flowing out, your handshake is just right!

Another situation when etiquette comes into play is when there is a meal involved. It's reported that 85% of business is conducted over a meal or a drink, so there's a good chance that some of your interactions with sponsors, clients and/or potential clients will involve 'breaking bread.' Most people don't stop to think about how they might be perceived while dining, so quite naturally, this is when most table faux pas are committed. Learning a few of the basics of dining etiquette will help you avoid doing things that might reflect poorly on you. Below are a few tips you will want to remember:

- The napkin should be placed in your lap the very minute you are seated at the table.
- Napkins go on the back of the chair if you need to leave the table.
- Keep pace with others at the table while eating. One sure sign that you're dominating the conversation is your plate is full when everyone else's is empty!
- Pass the salt and the pepper together- always.
- The proper way to eat bread is to place it on your bread plate, which will always be on the left side of your dinner plate. Place a small amount of butter on the plate. Break a bite

sized piece of bread off, butter it and place it in your mouth. Never butter the entire piece of bread and bite it.

- Your drinks will always be to the right of your dinner plate.
- Never blow on your food to cool it.
- Use the continental style of dining to impress VIP's; fork in left hand, knife in right.
- Dab your lips with the napkin after every 3 to 4 bites.
- Never use a toothpick or put on lipstick at the table.
- Work from the outside in when multiple utensils are present at the place setting.
- Don't push your plate away from you when you're finished.
- Your napkin goes to the left of the plate when you're finished and about to leave.

Remember that etiquette is all about respect and respecting the company you are with. Too often people worry about the wrong aspect of etiquette such as which fork to use, etc... Commit to making your best effort to follow the rules you know, and let the mistakes of others go. When you do, it's a sure way to be remembered as the guest everyone is happy to invite back.

Karen A. Thomas is a certified Etiquette Coach, Corporate Trainer and Speaker. She provides clients with techniques to build overall confidence and social grace. Karen appears on radio and TV and is a sought after Etiquette Expert. She resides with her husband Ken and her 3 children and 2 step children.

She is available at www.ctetiquette.com.

In addition to Karen's advice, I'd like to share some information about lectern etiquette. Some people think that the words lectern and podium are interchangeable - they aren't. On the other hand, a podium and a soapbox are basically the same thing; a box someone would stand on to deliver their speech.

A lectern is a tall stand fashioned after the style of reading desks originally found in churches. The top of the stand was slanted to support bibles, books, or the speaker's notes. Today, a lectern is the focal point of the stage. It won't be on every stage you stand on (unless you request it) but when it's there, there is a specific protocol you will want to be aware of.

When introduced as the speaker for an event, it is customary to walk up onto the stage and shake hands with the person who introduced you. This hand-shaking represents the 'passing of control' for the meeting or event and has its very own point of etiquette.

Many of the people introducing you will not be aware of it. What they will do is stand at the lectern to introduce you to the audience and then step away from the lectern to greet you with a handshake. Formal speaker etiquette dictates that the lectern is *never* left unattended. People who know about lectern etiquette will introduce you and stay behind the lectern until you arrive, shake your hand and then step away, thus passing the control of the audience over to you.

When your presentation has concluded, you can re-introduce the person who introduced you by using their name or simply saying "Madame Facilitator." You would remain behind the lectern until they arrive, shake their hand and then step away, thus passing control of the audience back to them.

While these nuances may seem a little stiff and strange, they are the standard for most formal speaking events. Lectern etiquette, as well as all the other etiquette tips covered in this chapter, won't always be followed at every event, but knowing and following the simple tips provided will help build your confidence and composure. Besides, it's always better to be prepared and not have an opportunity to use them, then to suddenly have an opportunity and not be prepared.

Chapter 28

Speaker Sponsorship

One of the toughest things to hear from a potential client is: "We love what you do and we'd love to hire you to speak to our clients, but we just don't have enough money in the budget to pay you." Sometimes it gets worse because they add: "Is there any chance you'd be willing to speak for free?" Because you're passionate about what you have to offer, you'll be tempted to say yes, but unless you have access to a source of unlimited funds, your budget constraints - and possibly your landlord - will put a limit on the number of times you can speak for free.

It's a tough situation because speakers share information that can truly benefit an audience. Fortunately, there is a new option that might help you get in front of an audience even when your speaking fee is a problem. It's called 'speaking sponsorship.'

To understand more about how this works, I reached out to Julie Austin, owner of Speaker Sponsor. Her website provides a platform for speakers to list who they are, what they speak about, events they are looking for sponsorship for, and what benefits they can provide a sponsor in return.

Her site also provides corporations, businesses, companies, etc. with another opportunity to get their brand in front of their target audience by sponsoring a speaker with the same target audience in mind. Here's what Julie has to say about this concept of speaker sponsorship:

If you're just starting out in a speaking career, there's one thing you'll eventually find a little frustrating. Many meeting planners are now asking speakers to speak for free. In the beginning that won't be a big problem. In fact, you should do as much free speaking at your local Chamber of Commerce or Rotary Club as you can to practice your craft. Those gigs are easy to get and you usually don't have to travel very far.

Once you start moving up the speaker ranks, it's natural to start thinking about making money. Public speaking may be exhilarating and rewarding, but it's still hard work and you'll be putting a lot of time and energy into it; you deserve to get paid. I can't tell you exactly when you should start charging, but you'll know when it's time.

Once you've made that decision, it's time to start negotiating with meeting planners. If they say they simply don't have the money in the budget to pay a speaker, you still have options. One option is to ask if you can get your own sponsor. I've never had a meeting planner say no. Why would they? They get a top speaker with great content, who doesn't sell from the stage, and they don't have to pay a penny. Instead, the sponsor pays the speaker for the opportunity to get their brand in front of the speaker's audience. It's a win - win for everyone.

The concept of sponsorship has been around for centuries, but corporate sponsorship is really still in its infancy. The idea of speakers getting corporate sponsors is an even newer application. That's good news for you because the market isn't oversaturated yet.

Here are 3 ways a speaker can get sponsored:

- **Get hired to speak for free at an event:** Unfortunately more and more meeting planners are telling speakers they don't have money in the budget to pay them. So, instead of turning the job down, you can accept and then look for a sponsor to back you. Ask the meeting planner to pay your expenses; it's the least they can do. Once you have your sponsor, your job is to make sure the sponsor's brand is mentioned everywhere your speech is mentioned. That might be on the organization's website, in their email campaign, on your own website, in your own email campaign, on the room signage, on the kiosks around the conference, mentioned in all of your press materials, in press interviews and releases, a mention onstage, and anywhere else you can think of. The point is to bring value to your sponsor's brand.
- **Create your own seminars and events:** Let's say you speak on the topic of home remodeling and you put together a seminar called "Remodeling on a Shoestring" in your community. A local hardware company or a hardware product manufacturer would probably be thrilled to have a chance to get their brand in front of your audience. You would promote them the same way you would a conference you were hired to speak at. An additional advantage for your sponsor in this situation is that you're in charge of the room and can do things like have contest givea-

ways and promotional product giveaways, all with the company's brand/logo on them.

- **Have sponsors contact you with their own event ideas:** Meeting planners quite often contact you based on the topics you speak on. In the Renaissance era, artists were commissioned to produce a piece of art based on the artist's style. The sponsor had an idea of what they wanted and hired an artist to carry out their ideas. This is the same principle. Only instead of being hired by a meeting planner, you would be commissioned by a sponsor, who would pay you for your expertise.

You'll quickly find out that you have to be an entrepreneur when it comes to running a speaking business. There's a lot of competition for paid work. But you can eliminate the competition by getting your own sponsors. There are literally millions of businesses out there willing to pay you for the chance to get their brand and message in front of a targeted audience. Then it's up to you to be the best speaker possible and deliver the most value for the money.

Julie Austin is an award-winning author, inventor, and multiple business owner. She's appeared on ABC, CBS, NBC, FOX News, along with dozens of other TV shows, in the Wall Street Journal, magazines, and on radio shows around the world. She's a "go-to" business expert, keynote speaker, and seminar leader in the fields of innovation & creativity.

Her website, www.SpeakerSponsor.com, is a

matchmaking directory between speakers and sponsors. The membership site also provides sponsorship training, along with special events and contests for members.

Chapter 29

Professional Tips for Getting Hired Again and Again

When I got my first paid speaking gig, it went well enough, but if I had known then what I know now, it would have been a lot less stressful. As with any business, there's a learning curve. My goal in this chapter is to share information about how you can better prepare for success right from the start of your speaking career.

Make it one of your goals to be as proactive as possible. Being proactive is a way to decrease the chances of things going wrong and increase the chances of things going great. Please note that I said 'decrease,' not 'eliminate.' Things can and will go wrong. But by being proactive and taking action when it's within your power to do so, you can improve the odds of things going in your favor and reduce the amount of stress you and your contact might be feeling before an event.

Preliminary Site Visits and Tests

If you can, arrange a preliminary site visit with your event contact. This will give you the opportunity to locate any connections you might need for your equipment. If you're planning on using some of their equipment, ask if the person in charge of their equipment can be there so you can go over the details of your plan together.

Sometimes when I'm hired by a school system to conduct a parenting lecture, they want me to present from the auditorium stage. During my preliminary site visit to one school, I discovered that the screen they were providing was a portable, tiny 4' by 4' screen. They had brought that one onto the stage because the giant motorized screen I would normally be using wasn't working. If I had been forced to project onto that tiny screen, the impact of the video segments I was planning to run would have been lost. In addition, the images in my PowerPoint presentation would have been channeled through the school's LCD projector which only had one working color - green! While I was trying to think of a solution for these problems, the projector's bulb blew out!

Fortunately, finding out about all these issues prior to the day of the event gave my client plenty of good reasons and enough time to get better equipment into the auditorium.

Doing a preliminary site visit also allows you to scope out the room from the perspective of where you will be standing when you deliver your presentation. Look around and check for physical/environmental complexities that might be a challenge to deal with.

A common challenge for me is the size of the room in comparison to the size of my audience. People sometimes have a tendency to gravitate toward the back of the room, and I've found that the physical distance between us results in them carrying on conversations during my lecture.

On one preliminary site visit, I discovered that I would be speaking in the school's auditorium which seated well over 1000 people. The event was for only 180 people and I knew that some of them would probably sit towards the back where they would be more likely to talk and less likely to listen and be engaged in the information being presented.

To deal with this challenge, I arrived early on the day of the event with a few rolls of brightly colored contractors tape. I used it to tape off the back section of the auditorium so that attendees would be more inclined to sit closer. It worked. This kind of tape is not very expensive and you can find it at your local home supply stores.

Even when the event is so far away that you have to fly to get there, make an effort to visit the site as soon as you can. One event I was hired to speak at was on the opposite coast and I spent the entire day flying and waiting in terminals. By the time I arrived at the hotel – which was also where I was going to be speaking the next day - it was very late. I asked the front desk to page security to let me into the room I was going to be speaking in so I could set up and test my equipment.

When I walked into the room, I discovered that the front of the room was all windows looking out over the city. The view was probably very nice, but I needed a wall behind me to hang charts and diagrams from. They were a very important aspect of this talk and there was no way to display them on the windows or the curtains if they were drawn shut. I immediately contacted facilities and they sent up a few employees to help me rearrange the tables and chairs so that I would have a flat wall behind me.

Sometimes your site visit will have to be on the day the event is scheduled. That's okay; just make sure you arrive early enough to give yourself the time to patiently check everything out. If there's still a lot of time left over, use it to relax or to get a cup of coffee. Early in my speaking career, I hadn't yet learned the benefits of making a preliminary site visit. Instead, I learned the lesson the hard way.

I was scheduled to speak to a group of parents in a city about a 2 ½ hour drive from my home. I planned my driving time so that when I arrived I would have enough time to set up, but because my set up time was so short, I hadn't planned on arriving more than about 20 minutes early.

Unfortunately, I didn't think to account for the time zone change that occurred when I crossed over a state line! Instead of arriving early, I was very late and because I was the only speaker, the audience had left and my contact was very mad. If I had known about the importance of a preliminary site visit back then, I would have arrived much earlier to make sure everything was in place, and I would have been the only person aware of my mistake.

One more benefit of seeing the facility in advance of your talk is that it gives you a chance to get comfortable with the space. I referred to the The 7 Habits of Highly Effective People, written by Stephen R. Covey in a previous chapter, but it's worth going over Habit #2 again. He writes about how important imagining the outcome is as a way of preparing for greater success and instructs us to *"Begin with the End in Mind."* Take the time prior to the start of the event to stand and move around your stage, calmly and quietly visualizing the end you have in mind. Doing this will help you create a great presentation before it even begins.

Use Checklists to Reduce the Stress

Sometimes when people are just starting their speaking business, they find themselves stressing the night before their event because they're still scrambling to pull everything together. When you're stressed, you're so much more likely to forget something important to the success of your presentation.

One of my biggest pet peeves is when speakers stand in front of their audience and apologize for not having some part of their presentation with them. I've heard speakers say things like "I wanted to share an important article about XYZ with you, but I left it at home." Or "I usually have an XYZ with me to demonstrate my next point, but I forgot to include it in my luggage before I left the house." There really isn't a good excuse for this type of forgetfulness, and the event coordinator won't be interested in hearing your excuses anyway.

One thing you can do to decrease the likelihood of leaving something important behind is to create an inventory checklist of everything you will be bringing with you to the presentation. It's too stressful to try and remember everything you'll be using off the top of your head. This packing list will help you stay calm as you pull everything together and almost guarantee that you won't find yourself at your event with some critical component of your presentation missing.

Another checklist you want to think seriously about creating is one that will help you manage the time leading up to the event more efficiently. It's basically a 'to-do' list combined with a timeline. You list everything that needs to be done and estimate how long it will take you to complete each item. In the beginning it's almost better to schedule twice as much time as you think you'll need. Once you have your to-do list, pull out a calendar and start calculating start dates and completion dates. With a well designed to-do checklist, you can effectively organize your time so that your presentation, equipment, and anything else you are planning to use are completed and ready to travel when it's time to head out for the event.

Carry Your Written Introduction with You

Your introduction sets 'the stage' for the rest of the audience's experience with you. That means you want your introduction to include enough information about you and your experience for the audience to believe they are about to hear from someone who knows what they're talking about. Unfortunately, the person in charge of introducing you usually has just one goal in mind – to get through the introduction and get off the stage as quickly as possible.

In my early years of speaking, I've had people read my bio off of the back of my book, I've had them read someone else's introduction instead of mine, and I even had one person walk to the center of a large auditorium stage and announce "I don't know a lot about our next speaker so I'll let him introduce himself." Fortunately, because these things have all happened to me, I'm able to share with you one great tip for avoiding the mistakes that sometimes occur when it's your turn to be introduced.

If you look at the example of the Speaker's Agreement in the appendix, you will notice that I provide an introduction for the person who will be introducing me. Some people will read it word for word, some will make their own adjustments to what I've written, and some will totally forget to bring it with them.

Remembering to bring a copy of your introduction with you to every event is the kind of proactive thinking that helps eliminate the stress of this critical moment when you are making your first impression with your audience.

Carry a Copy of Your Presentation on a Separate USB Drive

As speakers, there are times when we rely heavily on our computers. For some speakers, myself included, computers are an integral part of the presentation because we use them to display our content. Sadly, there are times when our computers refuse to cooperate.

At one out of town event I was in my hotel room preparing for a day long lecture. I had less than an hour to finish my pre-event check of my PowerPoint slides and get down to the grand ballroom where about 50 psychologists and therapists would be filing in to learn about my latest research on handling disruptive behavior in children. All of a sudden, my laptop shut down and wouldn't power back up.

In a panic, I rushed down to the hotel business center and used a desktop computer to search for emergency computer repair technicians in the area. I found one located about 20 minutes away and left a desperate message with my cell phone number and the hotel's address. Their office didn't open until 7:30 a.m. and my lecture was scheduled to start at 8 a.m.

At 7:45, I began to prepare for the worst - having to do my presentation without my PowerPoint. I was grateful that my participants had a workbook, but most of the information, videos, and exercises I had planned on using throughout the entire day were trapped in my PowerPoint presentation.

At 7:55, a technician showed up and took my laptop out into the lobby. I began my presentation right on time with introductions and going over the agenda for the day. I was subtly delaying the start hoping it would give the technician enough time to fix the computer.

At 8:20, the tech walked in, plugged my laptop in and started it up. The audience applauded, and I was very relieved. From that moment on, I've always carried a USB drive with my entire presentation backed up on it.

A USB drive is a small external drive used to store computer data/files, and it is a great way to proactively prepare for technology issues. It connects with a computer USB slot and is about the size of your thumb. In fact, some people refer to it as a 'thumb drive' or a 'jump drive.'

External drives vary in price according to the amount of storage they provide and you can purchase them at most stores that sell computers and electronics. Be sure the one you choose has enough storage capacity to hold all of your presentation. Then, if something happens to your laptop, you'll still be able to access your presentation once you have access to another computer.

Don't Let It Go To Your Head

Even if you've been hired as the headline speaker for a huge event, it's not a good idea to walk in like one of those inflated balloons you see in the Macy's Thanksgiving Day Parade. Designing, planning and pulling together an event is hard work regardless of how big or small the event is, and the person in charge is likely to be very busy when you arrive. They'll want to know you are there, but after that, the more proactive you can be about making sure you are set up and prepared, the better.

Think about the event from the planner's perspective. They asked you to speak because they believe you will be an asset when it comes to making their event a success. But making sure you have everything you need is just *one* of the priorities on their list. So when you get there, go in with the attitude that you are there to help the coordinator pull off a successful event. Think in terms of how you can be of service to them and avoid being one of those 'rock star' speakers that struts in with a list of demands.

Again, be proactive and be prepared with your checklist of things they've agreed to provide. This minimizes the number of times you'll have to interrupt the event coordinator while they're attending to all their other tasks. It's also a good way to grow your reputation as a professional who's easy to work with and improve your chances of being invited back.

Don't Sell From the Stage

This was mentioned in a previous chapter, but it's one of those speaking 'taboos' that's worth saying a little bit more about. People don't like being tricked and that's what it feels like to them when they attend a presentation that promised A,B and Ç, and then realized that all they were going to get was 'A.' If they want access to the rest, they'll have to give up their credit card info.

Most speakers know they aren't supposed to sell from the stage, but sometimes the monetary aspect of the speaking business gets in the way. When this happens, a speaker might be tempted to organize their presentation with almost all of the information the audience needs, and then sell the rest of it at the back-of-the-room sales table as a book, CD, DVD, etc.

Sometimes this transition is so subtle that even the

speaker it's happening to isn't really aware of it. It's just a challenge when you're getting started because there's such a temptation to think of the dollars coming in as a reflection of the value of your passion and your message. When your goal is honest and sincere, you want to share. That's what draws us into the business of speaking in the first place - to share something meaningful that will be of service to others. There's nothing wrong with wanting to be paid as part of the process.

The reality is that when you are passionate about the information you share on stage, your audience will run to that table at the back of the room to see what else you have to offer. Even when you share your best information, no one else will be able to deliver it the way you do and when your audience members crave to hear it again, or to hear more, they'll seek you out.

That being said, there are some very subtle ways to remind people that you have a lot to offer off the stage as well. As I mentioned earlier in the book, if you have a book, figure out a way to read something out of it. You don't have to tell them it's for sale, they'll see you holding it in your hand on stage and then they'll see it on the back table. If you are a coach, tell a story about a client you were coaching. If you offer training, tell a story about something that happened in one of your classes or with one of your students. You get the idea.

Sometimes, when you're done with your presentation, the same person who introduced you will come back up on stage to get the audience to thank you with their applause. They might be willing to remind the audience that you have products available at the back of the room too.

Get Permission or Give Credit Where Credit Is Due

At an event where I was hired as one of the breakout speakers, I had brought in a small staff to attend to my sales table so that I could enjoy the keynote speaker as well as some of the breakout sessions. I love attending keynotes; it's an exciting opportunity to learn from other great speakers.

The keynote for this event was a professor from a local university speaking on a very interesting aspect of human behavior. As her presentation progressed, I was very impressed and took lots of notes on the material and on things she did very well as a speaker.

But about half way through her presentation she lost all credibility with me by breaking a universal rule. She used someone else's material and didn't give credit to, or acknowledge permission from, the author/artist! In this case the material was a very funny comic that appeared as part of her slide presentation. She read the punch-line aloud and a majority of the audience immediately broke into laughter. She smiled contently at us, gratified by getting the laugh she had been hoping to get. I was hoping she would say something to acknowledge the artist, but she didn't.

I would have thought that a college professor would have known better than to use someone else's work without giving them credit. Apparently, she didn't. I can't say that she meant to intentionally deceive us; I don't know what her thinking process was. All I can speak to is the effect it had on my thoughts about her as a professional. I was no longer engaged in her presentation and really wondered how much of the material she was presenting was actually her work.

Some people make the mistake of believing that if someone else's work doesn't have the copyright words or symbol at the bottom of the material, then its fair game. Not true! According the Copyright Act of 1976, a copyright is created as soon as the material is created, written, filmed, recorded, posted, or saved to a computer hard drive. For example, there is no legal need for me to note © Bill Corbett 2014 at the end of my written words or on an image I've created. If someone else uses my work, they know they didn't create it. They know it belongs to someone else.

There are a few ways you can avoid this potentially disastrous situation. One way is to find the writer or artist and ask for their permission. I've used a lot of cartoons over the years, but have always contacted the artist to ask for permission to use their work. About 80% say yes. I've done the same with music and video clips. Then, at the bottom of the appropriate slide, I place a line of text that says "Used (or reprinted) with permission from _____."

When you can't find or locate the person whose work you'd like to use, you can decide not to use it or you can just acknowledge that it's someone else's work. It may take a little bit of effort to track down an artist or author, but I bet you'd appreciate it if someone made the effort to track you down before using your work and presenting it as theirs.

The Thank You Note

One of the greatest feelings in the world is successfully

completing your presentation. One of the most important things to remember about that moment is that it wouldn't have happened if it weren't for the person (or persons) that engaged you to speak at their event.

I cannot emphasize enough the importance of sending a thank you note to your event planner and/or the planning committee. Some people will be content to say thanks with an email, but how much effort does that take – almost none. But a hand written note expressing your sincere gratitude for having been provided with the opportunity to share your message on their stage will be one more reason for them to feel good about having chosen you to speak at their event.

Bits and Pieces

I probably could have written pages and pages of professional tips about things like: how to dress professionally, how to organize your time the day before an event, or to make sure you offer a good handshake while making eye contact when you meet your event contact for the first time. But this book is about getting started and giving you the information you need to begin your journey as both a speaker and a professional with a message to share.

There's a lot of common sense involved when it comes to dealing with people. Treat the people you are working for and audience that comes to listen to you with respect and you'll be on your way to building your good reputation as a professional speaker.

Afterword

I really enjoyed writing this book. When I first came up with the idea, it was just one of those projects you put on your list of things you'd like to do, but just don't know how you'll find the time to do it. But we now live in an age of information and people want to know about things, about how to do things, and they want to hear it from people who've 'been there and done that.'

There weren't any books like this when I started to build my speaking business in the mid 1990s; but that didn't make what I had to offer my audiences any less valuable. Today there are many people who believe in the value of what they have to offer and there are audiences who want and need to hear it. Stepping onto a stage is one of the most effective and rewarding ways for someone to share their message and their passion with a goal of helping others. I learned how to do it by trial and error; you don't have to.

In a recent radio interview, I was asked if I could identify one or two key characteristics that separate the truly professional speaker from the rest. I didn't even have to think about it, I knew exactly what those characteristics were.

The first characteristic is doing everything in your power to meet and exceed the promises you make to your meeting planners and event participants. Speakers can have the most polished of stage presences imaginable. They can have amazing stories and content to share. They can even be famous, but none of that will matter if they don't show up both physically and mentally.

Meeting planners and event coordinators have nightmares about their speakers not showing up for their event, and rightly so, it happens. Maybe you've attended a conference or event specifically to hear one speaker, only to find out that they had canceled at the last minute. I've had that happen to me and thought about asking the event coordinator what happened, but they were already surrounded by a group of unhappy attendees.

I'm not suggesting that speakers struggling with life altering or threatening situations show up to conduct their presentations anyway. Some serious situations do occur and taking care of yourself and your family does come first. I am suggesting that speakers assess their situations honestly.

Two days before I was scheduled to speak at a large early childhood conference, my teenage son and I were involved in a very serious traffic accident. Someone had made an abrupt and unexpected left turn right in front of me, resulting in my truck hitting them. The tremendous impact sent both my son and I to the hospital by ambulance. My truck was demolished. We escaped without any life threatening injuries, but were both severely bruised.

The next day I was in intense pain and seriously thought about cancelling my presentation. I knew it wasn't going to be easy, but I believed I could manage the pain and was even a little grateful to have something other than the accident to focus on. When the day of the conference arrived, setting up was very hard, but I managed and both of my customers – the event coordinators and the audience – were very happy with my presentation.

Being mentally present is just as important as physically being there. We all know what it's like to be in one place and be distracted with thoughts and ideas about being somewhere else, doing something else. It happens. When it does, true professionals bring their focus back to why they choose to be *here*. They connect with their passion and their message and then step on stage to share it.

Sometimes it's the challenges we face that help us remember why we chose the stage in the first place. When you make a commitment to be 'present' for your audience both physically and mentally, they are much more likely to connect with you and your material.

The second characteristic has to do with understanding your audience. This means doing the preliminary work to find out about the people who will be sitting in your audience. In my speaker's agreement, I ask them to tell me about the people I'll be speaking to. The more I know about them, like what they do for work, what their challenges are, and why they will be attending my presentation, the better job I can do of planning my presentation with their needs and expectations in mind.

I could tell you dozens of stories that reflect how beneficial learning about your audience before speaking to them can be, but I have an even better story of what happens when you don't.

While I was working at my first civilian job in a very large corporation, my project team and I were treated to a fancy wine and cheese party for the outstanding work we had done with a specific project. The small event was hosted in the company's exclusive business dining room. It was quite an honor, and we were all very excited about being recognized for our long hours and hard work.

We learned that the guest speaker for our event was none other than the company's president, and I remember the nervousness I felt in anticipation of meeting him for the first time. I was a young computer programmer and this was a very exciting event for me.

Without warning, a man in an impeccable dark blue business suit confidently strode in through a side door with an entourage of attendants in tow. He paused momentarily as one of them whispered something in his ear, and then after a few seconds, he strode to the front of the room and stepped behind the lectern. He looked at all of us with a big smile and said "I don't know what you people do, but they tell me you do it well."

Even as junior employee still wet behind the ears, I knew his remark was very inappropriate and unprofessional. He left us all feeling like our hard work wasn't important or meaningful. How could the company president be addressing this event and not know what we did for work? This was a life-long lesson for me to be sure that I knew my audience before I addressed them at the front of the room.

In this book, I've provided you with a plan for taking your passion and expertise and building a speaking business. I wrote it because I know you have something meaningful to offer. I also know there are people who really want and need to hear your information, ideas, insights and strategies. I've provided examples that illustrate my success as well as the successes of others, and I've provided you with a process you can follow each step of the way.

As you refer back to this book to keep your plan on

track, take time to record and acknowledge your successes; they build on each other. I also hope you will consider sending me an email or letter to share your successes with me. We are all the masters of our own success, but it's nice to think that my book might have helped.

Appendix

SPEAKER'S AGREEMENT
(speaker name)
(speaker address)
(speaker email address)
Cell phone and for emergency contact on the day of the event:
(speaker cell phone)

Thank you for the chance to be of service to you and the ABC Organization on (date of the event). The event is scheduled to begin at 9:00 am. I will be arriving the night before at the hotel your company will be providing for me. I plan to end my presentation at exactly 2:00 pm but would be happy to stay around afterwards for questions. Directions and a map will be greatly appreciated.

Please take the time to fill in important information below, sign it, and get it back to me via fax, email or regular mail. I will send a signed copy back to you as a confirmation.

(speaker name) Program Confirmation

Primary Contact Information
Primary Contact Name_____
Title:_____ _____
Work phone/extension: _____
Cell phone: _____
Email:_____
Phone # for emergency use only: _____

Invoice Information
Paying Organization Name:_____
Organization Address:_____
Organization Website:_____
Event Location Information
Location of the Event:_____
Address of the Location:_____
Room Name/Number:_____
Special instructions for parking_____
_____
_____

Hotel Information
Hotel Name:_____
Hotel Address:_____
Hotel Phone #:_____

Reservation Confirmation #:_____

Event Information

Start and Stop time of event_____

Lunch break time frame (if any)_____

As agreed, the topic I will speak on is: _____

_____

_____

Dress code for this event will be:

_____

Tell me three things I should know about this group?

1._____

_____

_____

2._____

_____

_____

3._____

_____

_____

I normally use fun and interactive role-play to help demonstrate key concepts to my audience. Please provide me with the names of 5 volunteers I can call on to help me with the demonstrations. I promise not to embarrass them or put them on the spot. It is my intension to seek them out prior to the event to brief them on what will happen.

1._____

2._____

3._____

4._____

5._____

What has this group been told about me or my presentation?

_____

_____

Here is some biographical information on myself that you may use to introduce me to the group:

Bill Corbett is the author of the "Love, Limits and Lessons" program, and the president and founder of the parent education organization *Cooperative Kids, LLC*. He provides parent education courses, staff training, and parent coaching to help reduce the stress that comes with raising children in today's world. Bill is a professional speaker and writer whose syndicated column on discipline appears in parenting publications in many states across the country. He has 3 grown children, 2 grandchildren and lives in Connecticut.

Fee Agreement

As we agreed, the fee for me to do this event will be $ _____. There are no additional travel fees at this price, but you have agreed to provide me with one night's hotel lodging for Tuesday, June 17. It would be appreciated if the check is available for me on the day of the event. It should be made payable to Bill Corbett. My federal tax ID, in the event it is needed, is _____.

Table Sales

To allow the participants in my presentations to take a piece of the event home with them, I often set up sales tables at the back of the room so they can purchase my books and tapes. It would be a great help to me if you were able to provide a volunteer who would be willing to handle the sales of my merchandise, so I can dedicate my time and attention following the event to answering questions for the group. Please provide that person's name here if you've selected them in advance: _____

Photography

Because I occasionally need to update promotional materials, this event may be captured as photographs, audio and/or video. Your initials at the end of this section give me permission to use those items in future promotional material.   Please initial here

_____

Sound

In the event that you are expecting a large crowd, or if the room has a high ceiling, I will require a microphone to improve the acoustics and help make this event a success. The microphone needs to be a wireless lavaliere/lapel microphone; a wired or hand held microphone is not an adequate substitute.

Room Setup

The room should be setup in a fashion that makes everyone comfortable. Your participants will be filling in information on my handouts, so a setup that is comfortable for them to write is best. You may also want to be sure and provide pens or pencils for those who may not bring one.

At the front of the room I will need two things: a white board or flip chart and a small table that I can work from. I would also like a table at the back of the room for book sales.

The following is a checklist of items mentioned in the agreement. Please check the items you are able to provide. If you aren't able, or have questions or need more information or clarification, please call me.

_____	*Flipchart with markers at the front of the room/on stage*
_____	*Table located at the front of the room where I will be speaking*
_____	*Table located near attendees entrance for book sales*
_____	*LCD Projector for PowerPoint*
_____	*Audio system I can connect my laptop to for PowerPoint/Videos*
_____	*Lavaliere/lapel microphone*

Referral Letter

If you are happy with my presentation, a letter of testimony on your organization's letterhead would be very helpful for my career as a speaker and trainer. I will contact you following the event in hopes of receiving the letter.

Thank you again for the chance to be of service!

_____
Speaker's Name

_____
Client's Signature

Sample Evaluation #1 - Formal

Session Date: _____

Rating System: 1=The Worst   2=Poor   3=Average   4=Good
5=Outstanding

About the Session: (please circle one)

1. Did this session satisfy your needs for professional develop-
    ment?

    1   2   3   4   5

2. Do you feel that the presentation kept you engaged and inter-
    ested?

    1   2   3   4   5

3. Do you feel it met some or all of your needs in understanding
    student/child behaviors?

    1   2   3   4   5

4. Did this session use multiple learning methods?

    1   2   3   4   5

5. Do you feel you will be able to use what you learned beyond
    your profession?

    1   2   3   4   5

6. What did you like most about this professional development?

    _____

    _____

    _____

    _____

7. What did you like least about this professional development?

    _____

    _____

    _____

    _____

Page 2

Rating System: 1=The Worst 2=Poor 3=Average 4=Good 5=Outstanding

About the Facilitator: (please circle one)

1. Did the facilitator appear to be well organized?
   1   2   3   4   5
2. Did the facilitator stay on time according to the session schedule?
   1   2   3   4   5
3. Did the facilitator use methods that were effective for your learning style?
   1   2   3   4   5
4. Did the facilitator encourage participation and questions?
   1   2   3   4   5
5. Did the facilitator help bring out new ideas?
   1   2   3   4   5
6. Did the facilitator know the material in the presentation?
   1   2   3   4   5
7. Did the facilitator present the material in a clear and concise manner?
   1   2   3   4   5
8. Did the facilitator keep the audience engaged and interested?
   1   2   3   4   5
9. Did the facilitator appear to be knowledgeable on the topic?
   1   2   3   4   5
10. Would you attend a session again, given by this facilitator?
    1   2   3   4   5

Your Comments on the Professional Development Session:
_____
_____
_____
_____
_____
_____

Sample Evaluation #2
Informal Evaluation Form

Your comments and suggestions are very important to me. Thank you for sharing them.

Rating System: 1=The Worst   2=Poor   3=Average   4=Good   5=Outstanding

How would you rate this workshop: _____ If less than 5, what would make it a 5?

_____
_____
_____
_____

How would you rate the presenter: _____ If less than 5, what would make it a 5?

_____
_____
_____
_____

How would you rate the material presented: _____ If less than 5, what would make it a 5?

_____
_____
_____
_____

If you could add or subtract something from the workshop, what would it be?

_____
_____
_____
_____

Other comments or suggestions:

_____
_____
_____
_____

Thank You!

References

Acuff, J. (2011). *Quitter: Closing the Gap Between Your Day Job & Your Dream Job*. Brentwood: Lampo Licensing, LLC.

Burchard, B. (2012). *The Charge: Activating The 10 Human Drives That Make You Feel Alive*. New York: Free Press.

Canfield, J., & Switzer, J. (2005). *The Success Principles: How to Get from Where You Are to Where You Want to Be*. New York: HarperCollins.

Comm, J. (2010). *KaChing: How to Run an Online Business that Pays and Pays*. New York: John Wiley & Sons, Inc.

Covey, S. R. (1989). *The 7 Habits of Highly Effective People*. New York: Simon & Schuster.

Dyer, D. W. (1989). *Real Magic: Creating Miracles in Everyday Life*. New York: HarperCollins Publisher.

Hakim, C. (1994). *We Are All Self-Employed*. San Francisco: Berrett-Koehler Publishers.

Hollander, I. R. (2013). *PASSION! How to Do What You LOVE For a Living & Wake Up The WORLD With Your Work*. Kindle: Hollander.

Levinson, J. C., Frishman, R., & Lublin, J. (2002). *Guerrilla Publicity*. Avon: Adams Media Corporation.

McCutcheon, M. (2006). *Damn! Why Didn't I Write That? How Ordinary People are Raking in $10,000.00 or More Writing Nonfiction Books & How You Can Too!* Sanger: Quill Driver Books.

Miller, F. E. (2011). *No Sweat Public Speaking: How to Develop, Practice, and Deliver Knock Your Socks Off Presentation With No Sweat!* St. Louis: Fred Co.

O'Neill, H. H. (2011). *Find Your Fire At Forty: Creating a Joyful Life During the Age of Discontent*. Garden City: Morgan James Publishing.

Ostrofsky, M. (2012). *Get Rich CLICK: The Ultimate Guide to Making Money on the Internet*. New York: Free Press.

Pausch, R., & Zaslow, J. (2008). *The Last Lecture*. New York: Hyperion Books.

Pink, D. H. (2012). *To Sell is Humna: The Surprising Truth About Moving Others*. New York: Riverhead Books.

Poynter, D. (2007). *Self-Publishing Manual: How to Write, Print and Sell Your Own Book*. Santa Barbara: Para Publishing.

Sather, C. (2011). *Dream Big Act Big: Breakthrough and Unleash the Superstar within You*. Danbury: Croix Sather Publishing.

Walters, D., & Walters, L. (1997). *Speak and Grow Rich*. Paramus: Prentice Hall.